SUPPORTED
SELF-DEVELOPMENT®

Linda —
You are a
true friend
thank you for that
and for liking the
book

David

SUPPORTED SELF-DEVELOPMENT®

HOW MANAGERS CAN USE THE SKILLS THEY ALREADY HAVE TO DEVELOP THEIR EMPLOYEES

BY

DAVID BERKE

david@supportedselfdevelopment.com

ISBN-13: 978-1-482314-65-6
ISBN-10: 1-482314-65-7

Library of Congress Control Number: 2013901934

CreateSpace Self-Publishing Platform
North Charleston, SC

Supported Self-Development® is a registered trademark owned by David Berke, Nancy Lorsch, and Deborah Pettry

Cover and interior text design by Gregory Smith

For Nancy

Also by David Berke

Succession Planning and Management:
A Guide to Organizational Systems and Practices

Developing Leadership Talent
David Berke, Michael E. Kossler and Michael Wakefield

INTRODUCTION

This book is for managers who want an easy to use method to support the development of their employees. This book is also for HR staff whose job includes helping managers to develop their employees. And although it is addressed to managers, this book is for anyone who wants an approach to helping people develop their knowledge and skills that is easy to understand and to use.

The book is called Supported Self-Development. That is because all development or learning is fundamentally self-development. I can't learn for you. You can't learn for me. But very few people can figure everything out on their own. They need various types of support. At work, that's a manager's job and it is essential.

The basic premise of the book is that most managers don't need to develop a new skill set, like coaching, to do this. Most managers already have the skills they need. What they might not know is how to apply those skills to employee development. This book shows how to do that.

What Are Those Skills?

They are knowing how to work with others to: set goals, formulate a workable plan to achieve the goals, engage in problem solving, and conduct status meetings to determine whether and what course changes are needed. These are basic project management skills.

With Supported Self-Development, the manager supports the employee's efforts to create and implement his or her development plan in about the same way that a manager would support an employee's efforts to create and implement a project plan.

The manager acts as project manager for the employee's development plan. The manager has primary responsibility for ensuring the development plan is established and for providing ongoing support during implementation. The employee has primary responsibility for actually creating the development plan, implementing it, and learning. Both the manager and the employee are accountable for the goals or outcomes they have identified for the project. As with most projects and assignments, the manager's level of involvement will vary according to how experienced and knowledgeable the employee is.

The purpose of supported self-development is to enhance or develop the employee's job-related knowledge and/or skills. This is accomplished primarily through development assignments. The purpose is not to increase the employee's personal self-awareness. That could be a side benefit; but it is something to expect professional coaches to facilitate not managers.

If you are interested in the principles underlying this approach to development, please turn to the end of the book.

Direction

In the following pages you'll learn about the steps in Supported Self-Development: what it is, why it is important and how to do it. Forms for your use are at the end of chapters where those forms are introduced. Blank forms are available at *www.supportedselfdevelopment.com.*

The goal is to make this material easy to understand and apply. That is the reason for minimizing theory, conceptual models and jargon. And that is the reason for using approaches that most managers already are familiar with—basic project management, as described above, and project planning tools, especially **SMART** goals.

About SMART

We will be using **SMART** in several ways. Here is a preview.

SMART stands for: **S**pecific, **M**easurable, **A**chievable, **R**elevant, and **T**ime limited.

Why use SMART? As noted above, it is a useful tool and many managers are very familiar with it. But the individual elements have broader application in areas we will be addressing in this book—areas such as preparing feedback, and establishing the following: a development goal, a development assignment and a development plan.

There will be some small additions to SMART.

To specify desired skill/knowledge level, an **S** is added to the development goal. The development assignment must engage the employee and also provide feedback and other support structures. An **E** is added for engagement; **ST** is added for structure and the letters are rearranged slightly.

The acronym grows from SMART to SMARTS to SMARTESST. But because most already know SMART, there really are only three additional elements to remember: **S** for skill level, **E** for engagement, and **ST** for structure.

The Six Steps in SSD are:

1. **Agree on who will do what:** clarify mutual expectations
2. **Choose the right things to work on:**
   a. Identify what needs to be developed
   b. Define the development goal
3. **Design the development assignment**
4. **Prepare the development plan and identify what to assess or measure in observable terms.**
5. **Implement the plan: Assess progress regularly; adjust the plan as needed**
6. **Confirm that the goal was accomplished. Identify lessons learned and next steps**

To help illustrate key points we will follow the discussions and activities of a manager, Joe, and his team: Susan, Kathleen, Ken, and Steve. You'll watch as they work through implementing Supported Self-Development.

CONTENTS

Chapter One

AGREE ON WHO WILL DO WHAT:
Clarify Mutual Expectations

With any project, the person implementing is responsible for certain things; the manager providing support is responsible for others. It is important to establish expectations and rules at the beginning.

Chapter Two

BEGIN TO IDENTIFY WHAT TO DEVELOP

People often have an idea of what to develop—e.g. better presentations, quicker decision making, etc. But frequently a clearer focus is needed. In this chapter you see how to identify specific development areas.

Chapter Three

DEFINE THE DEVELOPMENT GOAL

The focus on identifying what to develop continues. For most project plans, SMART goals are used. But because this is a development goal, S is added to specify the desired skill level. SMARTS is used to define the development goal.

SUPPORTED
SELF-DEVELOPMENT®

AGREE ON WHO WILL DO WHAT
Setting the Stage

Chapter One begins with Joe, the manager mentioned in the introduction, thinking about what to do with the development plan sections of the performance appraisals he needs to complete . . .

It was first thing in the morning. Joe sat and stared at the four performance appraisals on his desk. The development plans needed to be completed. And then the development was supposed to begin.

Joe agreed that development was important. Most of the people who worked for him certainly wanted to continue learning. Beyond that, there was just a lot he wasn't sure about when it came to development. People in HR told him he ought to build his coaching skills. But he didn't really have time and he wasn't sure what exactly he was supposed to do as a coach. He'd been to a few workshops and there was good information. But it all just seemed very complicated and a lot of work. In the workshops he heard about styles and other ways he was supposed to change his behavior. Some people called them steps; other people called them perspectives. There were even colorful diagrams. It sort of made sense in the moment. But that faded pretty quickly. Bottom line: It was ok; but it was just too much. He already had a job.

He knew he didn't see himself as a teacher. And the truth was that Joe really didn't know a lot about some of the things his people wanted or needed to learn. How would he teach them if he had to? How could he coach them? Besides, development sometimes seemed like a black hole. While he agreed it was a good thing, he wasn't sure his people were learning enough and he was concerned that they weren't focused on what they should be learning. Whatever the case, he knew that his employees were not learning fast enough.

In the past, he would give his employees the development plan forms to complete. They would complete the forms and then he would have a discussion with them. And after that, well . . . not a lot would happen until the next year's performance appraisal. During the year, Joe would ask about progress when he remembered or when one of his employees had a question. But that was about it. He wanted to do something different this year. But he wasn't sure what . . .

Getting Ready

Like Joe, many managers certainly know that development is important and, like Joe, many managers don't really want to be coaches—or teachers. Most don't have much time, their resources are limited and they don't have all the answers. Instead of trying to force managers down a road many do not want to go, let's step back and reframe the discussion. Let's build on what managers already know how to do. And let's remember that there is another person in this, the person who is supposed to be developing.

Joe looked at the development plan forms. They looked just like project planning forms: they had a goal, a schedule with implementation steps and milestones, and criteria to assess or measure progress. He also noticed a section that asked what the benefits of reaching the development goal would be: the business case. This way there would be a direct connection between development and results— the benefits of engaging in the development. Joe suddenly had an idea. He would build on what he already knew how to do—manage projects.

Implementing a development plan doesn't have to be very different than implementing any other type of project. So what does *managing* the project mean? A project manager usually does not get involved in the details and probably won't have all the answers. The details are the responsibility of the person implementing the project. There can be very complex projects but fundamentally the project manager does the following:

- Collaborates on formulating the initial plan and on any re-planning
- Ensures that there are necessary resources and support to accomplish the project
- Engages in problem solving to address current and anticipated barriers to progress
- Utilizes regular project status meetings to do these things and to keep track of progress, so that he or she can engage as needed

Picture a typical status meeting. The person in charge of implementation presents or discusses information on status. During the meeting the project manager listens, asks questions, challenges as needed, provides feedback and advice, etc. If the project manager did not do these things (and others) during the status meetings the project might go off track, lose money and fail. Because the project manager is ultimately accountable for results, he or she does not want that to happen.

Now picture a meeting between a manager and employee to discuss the status of the employee's development plan. Does the meeting progress in the same way as the status meeting described above? Often the answer is no—even though the same skills are required.

Unfortunately a learning or development situation often seems to evoke the traditional teacher-student relationship. With SSD, the assumption is that the employee, the project implementer, is capable of learning and taking charge of that learning. And that the manager is capable of managing and providing various kinds of necessary support and guidance; this happens either directly or indirectly.

Avoid Assumptions—Clarify Expectations

Joe sat back and thought about how he would get started with this idea: he would treat development plans as if they were projects. The employees would be in charge of implementing the projects and he would be the project manager. There were two things he needed to do:

1. *Explain that he wanted to treat development plans like projects.*

2. *Establish who was going to do what—what he ought to be able to expect of the employees and what the employees ought to be able to expect from him —just as in the beginning of any project. He knew that doing this reduced misunderstanding and conflict. And with less drama, people usually accomplished more.*

The first turned out to be easy. He simply explained that:

He wanted to help them develop.

He thought he could be more helpful to them doing what he knew how to do instead of trying to be a teacher or a coach—which he wasn't sure he knew how to do.

As for the second, Joe thought it would be easiest to meet with all his employees at the same time. The employees would brainstorm answers to two questions:

- *What should we reasonably be able to expect of Joe (my manager) during the development process?*
- *What should Joe (my manager) reasonably be able to expect of me during the development process?*

Joe would brainstorm answers to similar questions: what he should reasonably be able to expect of them and what they should reasonably be able to expect of him.

Then they would discuss their answers and come to an agreement on mutual expectations.

Joe knew they would revisit what they'd agreed to and most likely adjust it. But it was a good way to get everything on the table. Joe set the meeting and sent out the questions for his employees to think about before the meeting.

For this book, managers and non-managers were asked those questions.

Here are the answers we heard when we asked them what they should *reasonably* be able to expect from their manager during the development process:

employee expectations

- Express confidence that I (the learner) can do it
- Don't act like this is a waste of time
- Provide feedback
- Provide resources and introductions to people who can help, if needed
- Meet with me regularly to discuss how things are going
- If I'm stuck, don't give me the answer; help me figure it out
- Help me stay on track
- Arrange work expectations and/or schedule so that doing the development assignment will not lead to failure on the job
- Don't punish me for making mistakes so long as the mistakes decrease over time and I don't keep making the same mistakes.
- Do not believe that failure to learn something equals being a failure

And here are answers from managers and non-managers when asked what their manager should *reasonably* expect of them (the employee): ## manager expectations

- Believes he or she can achieve the development goal.
- If things are not going as expected takes the initiative to identify different possible solutions before coming to me.
- Will not waste my time.
- Willing to accept that resource limitations might alter the goal and/or plans
- Is motivated to accomplish the goal—and knows how to stay motivated
- Is realistic about how well he or she is doing: can assess progress on their own or with input from others
- Is able to provide accurate and up-to-date status reports on his or her development plan status
- Is able to accept feedback from me or appropriate others without getting defensive
- Knows that making mistakes is all right—assuming the mistakes decrease over time and the same mistakes are not repeated.
- Does not believe that failure equals being a failure.

- Manages themselves and their time so that they can do their regular work assignments in addition to the development assignment

Discuss To sum up, managers and employees appear to have complementary expectations of each other and each has responsibilities.

Managers most want to see employees doing what effective project implementers do: they take charge, are proactive problems solvers, know where they stand in relation to the plan and milestones, report on that status accurately, accept feedback, and accept that there are limitations in terms of time and other resources.

To manage or to lead? Employees/learners want managers to manage. They want the managers to: obtain resources and contacts that the employees could not obtain on their own, engage in problem solving with them—not give them the answers, believe they (the employee) can successfully implement the plan (accomplish the development goal) and that the goal is worth accomplishing. Employees also want the development goal and plan to be important enough that the manager is willing to devote time to regular progress reviews. Too many development plans are written only to check off a box on the performance appraisal. This wastes time and other resources and nurtures cynicism.

How do managers and employees make this happen?

Joe and his employees had a productive discussion. He was about to end the meeting when one of his employees asked an important question:

"We've made some important agreements," Susan said, "but we still haven't talked about how we're going to make this happen. So, how are we going to do that? I already know we need to have a good plan and measures. But that's not really enough, is it?"

"We're going to have to help each other be accountable," said Joe. "But I think you're right. There's probably more to it."

"Well . . . if you don't mind me thinking out loud," said Susan. "So here's an example. We said we didn't want you to give us the answers. You said you wanted us to take the initiative to come up with different solutions when we run into a problem. How do we make sure that happens?"

"For that one," said Joe, "I think it's a matter of just doing it. What I mean is I'm expecting you to come with solutions and you're expecting me to work with you, but not try to have all the answers—which I don't have anyway, by the way."

"Here's one that's a little harder," said Kathleen, another of Joe's employees. "We said we didn't want you to treat us like a failure if one of us failed at something. You agreed. So how do we do _that_?"

The conversation took off from there. Ken, another employee, said, "You have to set realistic goals and time frames instead of thinking you can become an expert overnight."

Susan said that even if you do that, you can still be treated like a failure if you mess up.

"So how do you know if you're being treated that way," asked Joe?

They thought for a minute. Then Kathleen said, "Well, it's like if you don't have confidence in us."

"You mean I should believe you can actually learn whatever it is we've agreed on," asked Joe?

"Well, yes," said Kathleen. "But more than that." She thought for a moment. "It's like there was already a mistake. You'd totally ignore the person or maybe only give them an assignment because no-one else was available. Stuff like that." She paused again. "Then it feels really personal," she said, "almost as if it has nothing to do with work. It's like the person can't do anything right."

Everyone was silent.

"Ok," said Joe, "Sounds like this is a lot more than me being disappointed or even angry that someone messed up. So what do we do to avoid that?"

Ken spoke up. "Well, based on what Kathleen said, it reminds me of that old saying about the difference between what people do and who they are. You need to separate the two."

"I guess if they're old sayings, they're still around because there's something to them," said Joe, smiling.

They discussed this more and in the end they agreed that everyone needed to focus on specific behavior—what people do—and resist the temptation to question everything a person did because that person failed in one area. But they also agreed that the person couldn't keep making the same mistake. He or she needed to figure out what to do differently and act on it.

Separating the person and the behavior became one of the principles they identified. That led to one more principle: being as specific as possible when setting development goals and when formulating feedback and giving it.

Let's summarize some of the key points from their discussion:

- Making their agreement happen really depends on Joe and his employees helping each other to keep to their agreement by holding each other accountable.
- Being realistic is essential. Only characters in a movie become experts overnight. To apply knowledge and skill effectively the employee still must practice what he or she has learned—whether it is an interpersonal skill or a technical skill. Workshops alone do not "fix" anyone and learning takes time and effort.
- Don't assume that because someone failed at one task he or she cannot succeed at any task. In other words, do not generalize from one event to everything a person does or might do. Fundamentally, this requires the ability to separate what the person does (their behavior) from who the person is. This last point, the ability to identify and focus on specific behavior, will be an essential element of defining development goals, pro-

viding effective feedback, and assessing progress and results. And as we noted in the introduction, it has a direct link to SMART.

Having talked through mutual expectations, Joe and his team were ready to move on to the next steps. They knew this wouldn't be the last time they talked about these topics, but they hoped that this would be a strong foundation for those discussions.

Chapter Two

IDENTIFY WHAT TO DEVELOP

After their discussion, Joe and his team felt pretty excited and wanted to get on to the next step, which seemed fairly easy to some of them. For example:

- *Susan had recently had some problems with a presentation she'd delivered to a group of suppliers, so she knew what she was going to work on.*
- *During his performance appraisal discussion, Steve received feedback that when he was leading projects (he was not yet a manager) he didn't delegate effectively, i.e. the work was not always completed per schedule. And Joe had heard and reported to Steve that those to whom he delegated didn't seem to always understand what they were supposed to do. This was complicated by the fact that they didn't report to Steve.*
- *Kathleen had just been on the job a few months and needed to learn more about the business.*
- *Ken was a different challenge. As he put it, "When you've been doing some version of the same job for ten years, there isn't much that's new. Not that I couldn't tweak some things around the edges. But it's better for Joe to focus first on folks who have less experience."*

Joe met first with Susan. She was sure she knew what she needed to work on, but then they began to talk.

"It's a good beginning," said Joe, "but didn't you go to a workshop last year to improve your presentation skills?"

"Yes," said Susan. "And they got better."

"So what's the problem?"

"Well I don't know exactly. Some people say I don't hold their attention very well—like in the meeting last week."

"What do you think that's about?" asked Joe. "I wasn't there, but I know your Power Points were great: lots of color, not too much to read, and some animation."

"Yeah, well . . . " said Susan. They were silent for a few moments.

"Let's stop for a minute," said Joe. "Are you certain you know what you're trying to accomplish?"

"I don't think so," said Susan.

"So how will you find out?"

"Good question," said Susan. "It's not like I can take a test, like in school."

"Ok, so how could you find out?"

"Well," said Susan, "I think the best thing to do would be to record my presentations and watch myself. I don't want to. It's awful. But that's probably the best way—and easiest. Almost everyone has a camera. But it's really uncomfortable."

"It's also a great idea," said Joe. "You can set that up for your next presentation. When is that? In five or six weeks?"

"Ok," said Susan.

"Do you want anyone to watch with you?"

"Do you mean watch the recording with me, or watch me present and then watch the recording—or both?"

"What do you think?" asked Joe. "You're supposed to be in charge."

"Well . . . I want to look at it alone first to see if I can figure it out. It's just so embarrassing, you know, and uncomfortable having someone else there."

"Works for me," said Joe. *"As long as you figure out what needs to change and how you're going to do it."*

"What do you mean?" asked Susan. *"If I'm doing something weird, I'll just stop."*

"Ok," said Joe. *"Let's say you're making weird gestures. You're not just going to stop all gesturing. What gestures would you make instead? Or what if you're still looking at the screen too much? What are you going to do instead? And how are you going to do it? See what I mean? That's going to be the development goal."*

"OK," said Susan. *"I'll set things up for my next presentation."* Susan then stood up to leave.

"Wait," said Joe. *"Are you forgetting about this last presentation?"*

"What do you mean?"

"Are you just going to wait until the next presentation? Aren't there some things you can learn from the last one? It sure sounded like it when we started."

"Looking at a recording just seems a whole lot easier and more accurate," said Susan.

"That could be," said Joe.*" But you won't always be able to do that. Besides, don't you want the next presentation to be better? Talking to some of the people who saw your last presentation might help you get some ideas on what to improve. It also could narrow your focus when you're looking at the recording."*

"What do you think I should ask them?"

"Let's talk about this together," said Joe. *"You have a general idea of where you want to focus. So what would you want to ask them?"*

"About their reactions, I guess."

"Ok. Here's a reaction," said Joe. *"I am very impressed. You were terrific. Is that enough information?"*

"Not really."

"Why not?"

"Slow down. You're putting me on the spot," said Susan. *"I need a chance to think."*

"Sorry," said Joe. *"But you know if you just walk up to someone and ask them about your presentation they might respond the same way."*

"You're probably right," said Susan. *"Listen, let me think about this. I guess I have to do some planning. Can we talk tomorrow or the next day?"*

"Sure," said Joe. And they set a time.

Identifying what to Develop

Identifying what to develop is usually a process of going from the general to the specific. Susan knows the general and needs to identify the specific(s). She might be able to identify the specifics herself by viewing a recording, but it is likely that she would benefit from conversation and input from others.

Susan's development process begins here—not with development plan implementation. She has the lead, not Joe. That means she has primary responsibility for determining what she needs to learn or develop. Having primary responsibility does not mean that she must do this alone. Like any effective manager, Joe should provide input and necessary resources, and arrange for meetings with experts and those who could help.

There is no absolute rule about how involved the manager should be in this process. The manager's level of involvement can and should vary in fairly obvious ways. For example, if the employee is inexperienced or a novice in the development area, the manager probably will need to be involved more or arrange with an expert to do that. If the employee is experienced in the development area, the manager probably will be less involved.

Whether the manager is involved a little or a lot in determining the development goal, he or she should be involved enough to:

- Be able to present a business case for the development project. It doesn't have to be long and complex. The manager ought to be able to justify the use of organization resources—just as a project manager would have to do with a project.
- Be sure that the development goal accurately describes whatever needs to be learned—especially if the manager is directing the employee to learn something. As project manager, the manager has overall responsibility for accomplishment of that goal.

We saw Joe help Susan think through how she could identify what she needs to develop and what she needs to consider further. As Susan's manager, Joe left implementation to her. Now Susan needs to consider how she will gather information from the people who saw her presentation, and then discuss it with Joe.

There are several methods for doing this. The ultimate goal of each method is to break a particular task into its component parts or *performance elements* so that the specific area(s) needing development can be identified more easily and then prioritized. Susan would use this list as the basis of her conversations with those who saw her presentation.

To the extent possible those performance elements should be written using behavioral terms or language. We will return to performance elements shortly. But first let's address behavioral language. It is essential for effective feedback and assessment of progress. We will refer to it many times in the following pages. Here's what we mean by behavioral language.

Behavioral Language

The nice thing about a recording is that you can just point to behavior—what someone says or does; you don't need to describe it. And if you have a recording, it certainly will make it easier to identify strengths and development areas. But often recordings are not

performance elements (handwritten note in left margin)

AVOID interpretation

available and obviously words are not a recording. When words are used to describe behavior, the same behavior can be described or interpreted quite differently. For example, what looks like *confident* behavior to one person, can look like *arrogant* behavior to someone else. When we say use behavioral language, we mean describe what someone does or says. **That's all.** No interpretations (like confident or arrogant).

watch trigger words

One client we worked with received feedback that he was too aggressive. He didn't disagree. However because he didn't know what he was doing that led to that conclusion, he didn't know what to change. Over time, he discovered that in meetings and other settings he often solicited input from others, but rejected almost anything that was different from what he wanted to do. People called this being aggressive. His behavior also could have been classified as not listening, or being arrogant, or being stubborn, or not being a team player.

Before he could determine what he wanted to develop, our client needed to know specifically what he needed to work on. That means he needed to identify the behaviors that he needed to change. As noted above, identifying the *performance elements* involved is an essential first step.

Methods for Identifying Performance Elements

The first method we'll describe is the traditional approach, task analysis. Then we'll describe the approach we recommend. We will describe two other methods at the end of the chapter: behavior modeling and using competencies. As a reminder, performance elements are the various skills and knowledge we use to perform something like delivering a presentation or delegating work.

Task Analysis

The traditional approach to a task analysis is to identify every step in a process. With all the steps identified, you determine which steps the individual needs to learn or improve. If there are several areas that need improvement, you prioritize and then select. If you are learning something technical, there is a strong possibility that at least some type of task analysis has been developed. If you are learning something behavioral, the training organization might have something.

Keep in mind that if you have to do a task analysis from scratch it can be a challenge. To illustrate the point, here's a little exercise: identify and write down all the steps needed to tie your shoelaces. Then give your write-up to someone and see if that person can successfully tie a pair of shoelaces by following your task analysis.

If you did this, you probably discovered that even though you are expert at tying your shoelaces, doing a task analysis on this simple and familiar task was challenging, possibly frustrating, and definitely time consuming. This is because being able to do something expertly is not always the same as being able to name and describe each step needed to do it.

Although it is the "book" solution, many will not have the patience to do a full task analysis. And, at this point, it's probably not essential—though ultimately it is necessary to know the details of what you will be learning. For now, what is necessary is to identify performance elements so that you can narrow your focus on what to develop or work on. And then, with specific areas identified, the analysis can continue.

Use Brainstorming

Brainstorming is an easy and often fun way to identify performance elements. The performance elements won't be in sequence or great detail. But for current purposes, that's ok. The rules for brainstorming are summarized briefly just below the example. Here are some performance elements Susan and Joe might identify:

- Voice can be heard at the back of the room
- Voice is not too loud—doesn't sound like shouting
- Voice is modulated to keep audience attention (not a monotone)

- The speaker varies the pace of speaking—doesn't speak too slowly or too fast
- Does not hesitate when speaking
- Looks at the audience
- Refers to slides but does not read them
- Uses gestures to emphasize key points
- No distracting arm movements, use of hands
- Facial expressions—appropriate to the content
- Uses clear language the audience will understand
- Varies the content so that the audience won't get bored

The list could go on. The point here is that brainstorming the performance elements might lead you to identify the development area. Or you might be reminded of other performance elements, one or more of which could also lead you to the development area. The challenge with brainstorming is to ensure that all the performance elements eventually are described in behavioral terms. We say *eventually* because you shouldn't worry about that when you are brainstorming the list

Here is a summary of the rules for effective brainstorming: *use for Brainstorming*

Do:	Don't:
• Go for quantity—the more ideas the better	• Get a few decent ideas and stop
• Welcome unusual ideas	• Play it safe
• Withhold criticism	• Evaluate immediately
• Combine and improve ("piggy-back")	

Choosing the Right Things to Work On

Joe and Susan decided to brainstorm the performance elements for delivering effective presentations and used the list described above in the brainstorming example. Susan decided to use that list in order to have brief conversations with several people who attended her last presentation. She simply explained that she noticed that parts of her last presentation didn't go as well as she would have liked and was hoping to get some input on that. Then she showed those past participants the list of performance elements she and Joe had brainstormed and asked them which she had done well and which she could have done better. She also explained that they didn't have to worry about her arguing or being defensive; she was just going to listen and ask questions if she didn't understand something.

The list helped the past participants remember elements of the presentation and after a few minutes, Susan usually was able to obtain some useful information. She said, "thank you" at the conclusion of each conversation.

It turned out there were several things that she could have done better but there were three related standouts:

1. She hesitated when speaking and answering questions
2. She tended to look down when answering questions—especially when the questions were difficult
3. Her voice got very soft and hard to hear

Taken together these performance elements led to the impression that she wasn't confident about what she was saying and perhaps was not very well informed on the subject. This really surprised Susan. She initially thought she hadn't made enough eye contact with the group—that she was reading the slides to them. Now she had a clearer idea of what to work on.

A More Structured Approach

Susan's approach was not as structured as some would prefer. If you prefer more structure, list the performance elements—the components of the task. After you gather your information—as Susan has done—rank those elements in terms of the employee's current level of expertise—low, medium, or high. Be sure to add to the list of performance elements if someone mentions one that is not on the list. Because self-perception is not always accurate, the employee and manager (or someone who is familiar with employee's performance) should do this together in whatever sequence makes sense.

Here is an example of a matrix you can adapt.

Performance Element	Current Expertise Level		
	Low	Medium	High
• Using clear language			X
• Does not hesitate when speaking	X		
• Looks at the audience		X	
• Uses appropriate gestures to emphasize key points			X

Generally speaking, the development target(s) would be the performance elements in which expertise is low—or lower than the rest.

When You Don't Know What to Develop

Joe has one employee, Ken, who doesn't really know what he ought to develop. Here are some questions he and Joe can use to identify potential development areas. Of course, these questions can be used with any employee.

- Are there recurring problems in the organization that could be addressed if this individual developed specific knowledge and skill to address those problems?
- Are there areas within the individual's job that he or she should do better?
- Are there current or upcoming changes (new technology, reorganization, etc.) the individual should know so that the organization and the individual will be better prepared?
- What knowledge and skills are highly valued in the organiza-

tion? Which are in short demand and therefore of value to the individual and organization?

* How could this person be prepared for advancement or to act as an interim replacement?

Summary

Before moving on to the next step, let's summarize what has been covered so far.

1. Identify the development area and desired outcome(s)—like the examples at the beginning of this chapter. Susan identified presentations, Kathleen needs to learn more about the business, Steve needs to find ways to delegate more effectively, and Ken still has to find a specific area.

2. Distinguish between an overall goal—like making effective presentations—and what someone needs to learn or develop in order to accomplish that overall goal. For example, there is no single skill/knowledge called "lawyer" or "engineer." Similarly, there is no single skill/knowledge called "holding the audience's attention." However, there are a variety of things you should know and/or be able to do to hold the audience's attention. For convenience, we call these *performance elements*. Here are several methods for identifying performance elements:

   * Task analysis
   * Brainstorming
   * Using competencies
   * Behavior modeling

3. Select one or more of the performance elements that have the highest priority for development.

Note: As mentioned earlier, here is the summary of additional methods for identifying performance elements. If you don't want to read it, please skip ahead to the next chapter.

Additional Methods for Identifying Performance Elements

Using Competencies

Competencies identify the knowledge, skills, and abilities (KSAs) needed to perform the primary tasks in a job. Joe and his team might ask someone in HR if they have competency statements for particular development areas. Many organizations use competency statements. Chances are someone in the HR department has a list or lists of competencies. If not, they are easy to find online. One thing to be aware of is that competencies are written for application in a variety of organizations. Because of this, they are considered to be generic and might require modification to fit a particular job or task.

Like the list you developed by brainstorming, a competency list might provide the specific competency you are looking for. But if it doesn't, it might help you think of the one you are seeking. Here is an example that applies to decisiveness. (Adapted from a competency developed by the Center for Creative Leadership)

Decisiveness

Prefers quick and approximate actions to slow and precise ones in many situations

- Does not hesitate when making decisions
- Does not over-analyze a decision
- Is able to choose among multiple options

An advantage of using competencies is that they are written in behavioral terms. Notice that this example provides clear and fairly specific behavioral descriptions of key performance elements. You would be able to see behavior that would tell you if the individual were being decisive. These descriptors might apply directly to an individual or they might help the individual and his/her manager to be more specific or to identify other elements that might be closer to what needs to be worked on. For example, someone might hesitate when making decisions because he or she needs help with prioritization. Or, he or she might have difficulty determining who is essential to consult and who isn't; they might be a perfectionist or have analysis paralysis.

Competency statements also can address knowledge. Here is an example that would be appropriate to Kathleen's development area.

Seeks Broad Business Knowledge

Has an understanding of the business that goes beyond his/her work unit; seeks to understand the financial aspects of the business and its products and services

* Has a solid understanding of products and services
* Knows how the various parts of the organization fit together
* Knows the business
* Understands the financial side of the business

A brief discussion on any of those topics would tell you whether Kathleen had knowledge in those areas. Or one of these areas might point to something more specific for her to focus on like: understanding certain products and services, or knowing how the organization fits together in terms of certain approval processes, or who reports to whom, etc.

Behavior Modeling

Seeing someone actually perform what you want to learn can be very helpful. The performance could be something live or recorded and could include things like making a presentation or a customer service representative handling a difficult call. Learning this way is called behavior modeling. You also could call it copying someone else's behavior. It is a form of learning that all of us have used from earliest childhood.

A model or demonstration helps the manager and employee to:

* See and/or identify the desired behavior instead of trying to

describe it, which can be difficult. That is because all the performance elements are—or can be—visible. (An expert sometimes can see things that otherwise would be missed.)

- Compare what the employee does with the model. This helps the employee and manager to see very directly what the employee needs to do, or do differently, and how.
  —This also eliminates the need to engage in lengthy analysis of what the employee needs to learn. Instead, point to the desired behavior and have the employee work toward that.
- Have a common reference point. Also the role model might be available to answer questions

A more focused variation of this approach is to perform the task in front of an expert. Then have the expert provide feedback on what worked and what needs to change.

Now that we have briefly reviewed alternative methods for identifying performance elements, let's turn our attention to establishing the development goal.

Chapter Three

ESTABLISHING THE DEVELOPMENT GOAL

Joe thought it would be a good idea to get the whole group together to discuss and agree on how they were going to define development goals.

Joe said that he wanted to keep things as simple as possible. He suggested using SMART goals to start, mostly because they already used them for project planning. Also, the SMART criteria fit other parts of the process. For example, when you give feedback, you have to be specific. And when you prepare milestones they need to be specific and measurable or assessable.

For the sake of clarity, here is how Joe and his team understand this type of goal:

S : specific

M : measureable or assessable

A : achievable

R : relevant (some people say that R stands for realistic)

T : time-limited

"OK," Joe said to the team. "Let's work through SMART just to be sure we're all on the same page. Ken what's an example of specific?"

"Well, like we said about feedback, it ought to be very concrete. Something you can see or hear."

"So for my development goal," said Susan, "what if I said my goal was to not hesitate more than three times in a 15 minute presentation?"

"So Ken, what do you think?" asked Joe?

"A few things," said Ken. "First, it sounds more like a measure of progress. I guess hesitating is a behavior so not hesitating is something I ought to be able to notice too. But the statement sounds more like a milestone. Second, I'm not sure I know the difference between hesitating and pausing. I mean I don't see anything wrong with pausing to collect your thoughts."

"Wow, I hadn't thought of that," said Susan. "I sort of have a feeling about the difference, but I'm not sure how to describe it."

"Ok. I'm not sure what Susan's going to work on," said Joe. "But it sounds like we're clear on concrete and behavioral." I'd like to try working through an entire example? Steve, would you be willing to use your development area for this?"

Steve thought for a few moments and then said that he'd rather not. He wanted time to think about it first. Then Joe smiled, turned to Susan, and asked her if it would be ok for the team to use her development goal as a learning exercise.

"Sure," she said. "I've already learned a few things. Besides, everyone already knows what I'm working on."

"OK," said Joe. "We'll come back to Susan's goal. Let's discuss the other elements and then see how they would apply to what Susan is working on. We've already begun to talk about measurement, so let's start with that."

"It seems to me that measurement is about counting," said Steve. "I see how that would work with milestones, but I'm not sure how much it matters if Susan hesitates or pauses two times or three times or whatever. I don't think that's really the point."

"Ok," said Susan. "So in this case, maybe measurement ought to be called assessment and we'll be looking at behavior. Are people actually doing or saying what they're trying to do or say.

Everyone agreed. As for the other elements in SMART, here is what the group decided:

<u>**A**chievable</u> means more than just being able to accomplish something. It's easy to set a goal that can be accomplished. In the context of a development goal, achievable really means <u>achievable challenge</u>. If it's not a challenge, if it's too easy, you probably aren't learning much and you might get bored and quit. Of course it shouldn't be too challenging—then you might quit because you don't think you can do it.

<u>**R**elevant</u> means relevant to the individual's on-the-job learning needs. People are much more likely to be motivated to learn something they *need* to learn to improve performance in their current job or prepare for a future opportunity. For a new employee, like Kathleen, most information can be very relevant and helpful. However, with experience, learning needs tend to become more specific to the individual and stop being one- size-fits- all. Ken is an example of this type of employee.

<u>**T**ime-limited</u> means simply that there must be a clear beginning and deadline for completing the goal. This also applies to the project plan's milestones.

Making it SMARTS

Joe thought they were finished, but then as he reflected on what Kathleen needed to learn it occurred to him that they hadn't discussed how knowledgeable or skilled someone should be as a result of the development. *"For example,"* he said, *"much of what Kathleen is developing is familiarity not expertise. And that's ok."*

Susan jumped in to the conversation and said that she wasn't trying to be a professional presenter. It wasn't her job and anyway it would take too much time to do. For now she was looking for a level of expertise where she could get her message across without distracting the audience or undercutting the message.

Joe added an **S** to SMART. The second S stands for skill or knowledge level, which means:

Not every job requires high levels of expertise. In some cases, familiarity or knowing where to look for an answer might be enough. Where high levels of expertise are necessary, recognize that it will take time to develop someone and that usually requires a willingness to invest money and possibly other organization resources. In contrast, an employee wanting to develop his or her expertise beyond what is needed may be admirable but not necessarily eligible for organization support.

Joe summarized their progress in a table:

The SMARTS Development Goal
Specific and behavioral
Measurable or assessable
Achievable challenge
Relevant to what the person needs to learn
Time bounded—there is a deadline
Skill or learning level identified

Joe suggested they try Susan's development goal. Susan began by saying that although the feedback she'd received was that she hesitated, tended to look down when answering questions, and was hard to hear, she didn't think she should work on those behaviors.

When Joe asked why, she said *"Ken got me thinking. The fact is I know how to speak and answer questions without hesitating or looking down. And I certainly don't always speak softly—as all of you know,"* she smiled. *"So I don't need to learn how to do those things. I didn't realize it, but I guess I was nervous or maybe I wasn't confident enough.*

"That makes sense," said Ken. *"In my experience the best way to deal with that is to practice a lot. Also, see if you can come up with as many questions as possible you think someone might ask you. And then come up with the answers to those questions."*

"I already practice," said Susan. "But that second point is great. I don't do that enough and then I get surprised."

"Ok," said Joe. "So what would your development goal be?"

"Well, following SMARTS like we talked about," said Susan:

*"**S**pecific: how about identify at least two questions and their answers for every major point in my presentation.*

***M**easureable is pretty clear: two questions and answers for each major point.*

*It's **a**chievable. It's **r**elevant. It's **t**ime bounded—I have to get it done before my next presentation. And the **s**kill/knowledge level is clear. What do you think?"*

"It sounds good," said Joe. "But having two questions as the measure bothers me. Isn't that just counting like we said before?"

"Not really," said Steve. "Two is kind of arbitrary. It could be three or four. As I understand what Susan is doing, she's just saying she wants to be able to comfortably answer more than one question about the main points she's making."

"I think I understand now. We should add a short version of what you just said so there wouldn't be a question about it," said Joe. "The assumption is that if she's prepared well enough, she won't do the looking down and hesitating and so forth."

At this point the conversation began to shift to other topics. Joe set a time to meet with Susan to talk about next steps. He also set a time to talk with Steve about his development goal.

Summary

The development goal focuses on developing certain skills and knowledge that will enable an individual to accomplish the broader goal. For Susan, it was developing and being able to give answers to what could be difficult questions.

The next step is to write the goal in terms of the SMARTS criteria:

- Specific and behavioral—can you hear it or see it
- Measurable or assessable outcomes—can be behavioral; if you need to count or use numbers make sure the numbers are meaningful
- Achievable *and* a challenge
- Relevant to the individual's learning needs
- Time bounded
- Skill or knowledge level defined

Other Key Points

- The development goal(s) should focus on only one or two performance elements at a time. While it's often easy to know what you want to develop, actually being able to do it can take concentrated effort over a period of time. If you doubt this, think about the last habit you tried to change.
- People have lots of experience at making assessments; on any given day they typically have to assess things like how long it will take to get into the office in the morning, or what chicken to pick out at the grocery store for dinner. But most people are not skilled at assessing themselves accurately. This is because when we are engaged in doing something, it is difficult to observe ourselves.
- If the employee overestimates his or her abilities and does not recognize that he or she needs further development, the manager should ensure that the employee receives appropriate feedback that provides evidence of the development need. For example, if the development area relates to presentations, the manager can show the employee a recording of a recent presentation.
- Whatever the development goal is, it should be important enough to the learner that he or she will keep going when things get difficult. Toward this end, it is important for the learner to know what he or she does to stay motivated and be able to apply

it to this development situation. Sometimes motivation comes simply from knowing that what he or she is learning is a real task which they will be evaluated on.

- Just as the development goal should be important enough to the learner that he or she will stick with it, the entire development effort should be important enough to the manager that he or she will schedule and hold regular meetings with the employee to support the development. There are at least two reasons for this:

  1. The employee's development is an investment of organization resources. Effective use of those resources is the manager's responsibility. The employee should be learning something he or she needs to know in order to accomplish a real job task or to prepare for a real job assignment. Both the employee and manager should know the business reason for the development effort.

  2. If the manager does not provide adequate time and support for the employee's development, the manager is sending a clear message that development is not important—to the manager and possibly the organization. In such circumstances, engagement and retention could become issues.

FORMS

Evaluating the Development Goal

1. What performance element did you select?

_____

2. Write the development goal which addresses the selected performance element:

_____

_____

_____

3. Evaluate the development goal to ensure it addresses all the criteria for an effective development goal. Use the grid below and place an X in the column which best describes whether your goal meets the criteria.

Criteria	Yes	No
• Specific		
• Measurable or assessable		
• Achievable; appropriate challenge		
• Relevant to the individual's learning needs		
• Time bounded		
• Skill or knowledge level		

Chapter Four

DESIGN THE DEVELOPMENT ASSIGNMENT

"Alright Susan, you've got the development goal. Time to put something together," said Joe.

"Ok," said Susan. *"The main thing, I think, is to identify some hard questions and figure out how to answer them brilliantly. I'll put together a plan."*

"Ok," said Joe as he got up to leave, *"let me know when you've got something to talk about."*

STOP!

This is often what happens after the development goal is identified: the focus on development and real planning for it ends. There appears to be the belief that, having identified the development goal, it will be easy to know what to do to reach that goal and that whatever is chosen will be effective. That belief is expressed when the manager makes vague and minimally useful suggestions like, "Why don't you go talk with HR about a workshop." Or, "Why don't you go talk with Evan. He's usually got interesting projects."

When you are managing a project, you want to create conditions that will increase the chance of its success. If there are some tight procurement deadlines, for example, you probably want to do more than hope everything arrives on time. The same principle applies to development assignments. The development assignment and its implementation are the link between the development need and the development goal. You can and should be intentional about selecting the activities needed to accomplish the development goal. This process has two parts:

1. Identifying possible development activities/experiences
2. Selecting those that appear to provide the greatest possibility for success.

Identifying the development activities/experiences

A development assignment is a series of activities or experiences which, when taken together, enables someone to reach their development goal. In project planning terms, they are called the "subtasks." As a side note, when you know the activities you are going to pursue, a significant portion of the development plan will have been written (but much remains: like the schedule, accountabilities, resources, etc.).

Identifying possible development activities is similar to identifying performance elements. That is because one of the questions you are answering about development activities is the same as the question you ask to identify performance elements: *What skills and knowledge are needed to do this?* But you must also ask an additional question: *What activities/experiences will help me to develop the knowledge and skills?*

We have already answered the first question. For Susan the specific elements she wanted to address related to hesitating, looking down when she answered questions, and speaking too softly. But Susan already knows how to speak loudly, etc. She speculated that the possible underlying reasons for her behavior had to do with not feeling sufficiently confident—something she intends to address by identifying difficult questions that could arise during her presentation and being prepared with their answers.

With regard to the second question, one way to identify development activities is for the employee to talk with people who have learned whatever the employee is currently learning. The manager can support that effort by arranging for an introduction, if needed. As we discussed in chapter three, brainstorming is another way to identify development activities.

Whether you are a manager or employee, when you identify development activities we encourage you to include the default solution, workshops and classes, and then move beyond it. Workshops and classes are useful for getting started. They also are useful for helping someone make the most out of a development experience by, for example, helping the individual know what to look for and to understand what is happening. But most learning occurs through experience not in a classroom. There are ways to categorize development experiences that may help you consider and select a variety of activities.

Experiences that lead to learning: 70-20-10

Research tells us that approximately

- 70% of learning comes from *challenging assignments and life experience*
- 20% comes from other people
- 10% comes from classes and reading

To help identify various development activities/experiences, on the facing page there is a list of possible development activities organized in terms of 70-20-10. The list is not all inclusive. The manager and employee can use it as a starting point for brainstorming potential development activities for the particular development goal; or they can brainstorm without using the list.

As a check on yourself, we encourage you to select a mix of development activities from the three categories. A blank 70-20-10 form is provided at the end of this chapter for your use.

70—20—10: Development Experiences/Activities

70% Assignments, Application, Experience	20% Other People	10% Traditional Learning Approaches
Practice & Participate: • Private & public rehearsals, group rehearsals • Role plays, practice sessions • On-line games, simulations • Real events **Perform & Produce:** • Action Learning, task team assignments, jobs • Presentations, leading meetings • Analyses, revisions, adaptations, innovations, original works • Mentoring, teaching, coaching **Get meaning from the experience:** • Debrief, Plan next application • Journal	**Observe, interact, and share stories with others:** • Peers, direct reports, colleagues elsewhere • Mentors, coaches • Managers, executives • Master performers • Job shadowing • Social networks • Blogs • On-line forums and bulletin boards	**Attend or attend to:** • Presentations, speeches • Workshops, classroom, webinars • Online courses, podcasts, recordings • Conferences, conventions • Movies, plays, reenactments • Competitions, tournaments **Read:** • Magazines, journals, articles, books

Selecting Development Activities and Assignments

"There are a lot of things to choose from," said Susan. "How do we decide which are the best things to do?"

"Why not just choose a few things," said Ken. "I mean, I'm sure you've already thought about some things you could do. Why waste time?"

"Sure. I've been thinking about it," said Susan. "Mainly, I think, I need to identify tough questions and come up with good answers. Brief ones, otherwise I'll lose the audience."

"So how are you going to do that?" asked Joe. "That's the development assignment part. Read a book? Sit in a room by yourself and come up with that stuff? Ask some people?"

"Those sound good. But I thought I'd start with just trying to come up with questions on my own first."

"Anything else?" asked Joe.

"I thought I'd talk with you. Try to role-play with everyone—stuff like that."

"How confident are you that you'll be fully prepared after you do those things?" asked Joe.

"Well," said Susan, "not completely."

"Is that another way of saying you're not?" asked Joe.

"Yes" said Susan. "I guess I'm not."

Joe turned to Ken and asked, "So what else do you think she should do? Steve and Kathleen, please join in too."

"It's hard to surprise yourself," said Kathleen. "I think you could have a hard time coming up with the kind of questions you want. So asking other people would be good."

"Maybe even asking them about what you're going to talk about," said Steven.

"Yeah," said Ken. "Get their input first. Then they won't be surprised and you won't either."

"Hold on," said Susan. "Slow down. I do get their input before I start. I'm not stupid. But instead of starting with a kind of blank slate, I could have

maybe a draft or something to talk over—not a dry run exactly, but something to talk about."

"That sounds good," said Joe. "I was thinking of something like that but you beat me to it."

Not all development activities are equally effective. The question is: what will work best for the specific employee and situation? After further discussion with the group, Susan had identified several development activities including:

- Reading books and/or articles to help anticipate key issues, questions, and answers
- Soliciting input and questions from two to three people in her potential audience before she finalized a presentation
- Preparing a dry run presentation
- Conducting and recording a dry run with co-workers, who would be given the presentation in advance so they could identify difficult questions to ask during the presentation
- Reviewing the recording of the dry run so that Susan could review her answers and delivery and then modify each and the overall presentation as needed

Before the meeting ended, Joe said that while identifying the development assignment was a good first step, he still wanted to identify criteria for selecting development assignments. He did this so that he wouldn't have to do it each time he or anyone else on the team wanted to assess development assignments. (It really doesn't matter whether you use the criteria to evaluate already-selected assignments or use them to generate a list of possible assignments.) Since these were Susan's development assignments, the group suggested that Joe and Susan talk about the criteria first.

"I'm ready," said Susan. "I bet you want to use SMARTS."

"Why not," said Joe. "It's easy to remember."

"Ok," said Susan. "Well I'm not sure there's enough."

"For example?" said Joe.

"Well let's take the development assignment about reading books and articles," she began. "We probably need something about staying engaged because reading books and articles is really not something I like to do. It feels like I'm not working. Anyway, that's not part of SMARTS."

"So what's with that word engaged?"

"I don't know," said Susan. "It's this HR word I keep hearing. But I do probably need to do it."

"Just curious," said Joe. "You're probably right. We'll deal with that. But let's look at what fits first. There might be other things too."

"Well," said Susan, "it's specific. I probably can come up with measures or ways of assessing. Based on what we talked about before, they need to be better than just figuring out how much I've read. It's an achievable challenge—more challenge really, like I said, since I don't like doing it. It's relevant—or I need to make sure it is. Otherwise there's no point. It will be time bounded. I don't want this to go on forever. Besides, I've got to deliver a presentation in a few weeks. And I'll want to do something at the right skill level. I guess I mean if it's too basic that won't work for me or my audience; it also won't work if it's too abstract and academic."

They talked about solving the assessment problem and engagement problem. As they talked, the solutions for both seemed to merge. Susan and Joe agreed that before selecting material to read, Susan would identify several questions she wanted to answer—or at least get information about them. The *assessment* would be about her ability to answer the questions and to find material that would enable her to do that.

They decided that having specific questions to answer would increase the likelihood that she would engage more in the process—though it did not guarantee she suddenly would begin to enjoy doing this type of work. Some of the questions would come from people she planned to interview and some would come from her own experience.

They agreed that *engagement* ought to be added to the list of criteria. Then Susan brought up another of the assignments—recording the dry-run and then reviewing the recording so that she, and possibly others, could assess how she handled the presentation by focusing on her answers and her delivery. This one seemed to fit all the criteria, including the one they just added, engagement. It was specific. Doing the dry run and then watching the recording were achievable challenges and certainly engaged her attention and energy. The recording provided a means of assessment and it was relevant to her goal. She admitted it probably would be important to have a deadline which would ensure that she would have to watch it. And she certainly was going to be checking for the skill level she was demonstrating.

But there was an additional element or criterion that seemed to be missing. Susan pointed out that when she talked to people who attended her presentation she was getting feedback from them. And reviewing the recording was also a way for her to obtain feedback. And so she thought that getting feedback ought to be included into the development assignment.

"Good catch! Feedback mechanism: you're right," said Joe.

Joe paused then said, "You know, I was just thinking about when I was new here, just learning—like Kathleen. You need some kind of feedback like we've been talking about. But sometimes you need more than just someone pointing out what you could have done better or something like that."

"I think I see what you're saying," said Susan.

"I'll give you an example," said Joe. "If mechanics have to fix something really complicated they usually have a long check list or list of procedures with them that they have to follow—even if they've been doing the same work for a long time. It's like having built-in feedback to help you figure out what to do if no-one is there to ask."

"I see," said Susan. "Or like talking something over with someone who's an expert. It's another way of getting guidance."

They both were quiet.

"Well I'm not sure what to call this," said Joe, "or how we fit it and engagement into something like SMARTS."

*"Let's see what the rest of the team says next time we talk about this,"
said Susan.*

When they eventually got to this topic in their next staff meeting, both Joe and Susan described their conversation and why they were suggesting adding engagement. She described the other criterion this way:

"We started off with feedback, but then we realized it's more. If you are learning something new or complicated, then some structure is needed for support to provide guidance or feedback that will help you stay on track and see how you're doing. A procedure is one example, another would be someone guiding or providing frequent feedback. Obviously, the more skilled you are in the area you are developing skills, the more targeted and less frequent this structure needs to be."

"You're calling it structure. So why don't we call it structure," said Kathleen.

"Sure. Makes sense," said Ken." It provides support."

"OK," said Susan. "So do we have to have a separate thing for development assignments or can we fit this in with SMARTS some way?"

"It's really just two more things," said Steve, "structure and engagement."

"I think we ought to build on SMARTS," said Joe. Then he noticed Kathleen writing something and asked if she had the solution.

"I have one solution, anyway," she said. "Take a look." She turned to the whiteboard and wrote:

"SMARTESST"

*"We keep SMART and move the **S** for skill level. The **E** is for engagement and the **ST** at the end is for structure," she explained.*

*"Well, said Susan, "remembering the word smartest should be pretty easy, even if it does have an extra **S**. Always nice to see some real creativity. Thanks."*

"I guess the other way to remember it is SMARTS plus engagement and structure," said Joe. "The acronym really isn't the point. But I bet we won't need to add anything else to this."

"I hope not," said Susan and joked that she hoped they had enough *SMARTS* to be *SMART* enough to stop with *SMARTESST.*

"Ok. Ok," laughed Joe. *"Let's move on."*

Let's summarize. For a development assignment to be effective and successful it should meet certain criteria. To capture these criteria succinctly, we are using the acronym **SMARTESST**.

- **S**pecific
  Clear purpose and outcome in concrete and/or behavioral language
- **M**easurable/Assessable
  Can be behavioral; quantitative must be meaningful
- **A**chievable challenge
  Achievable but stretches the employee beyond usual performance level
- **R**elevant
  Applies directly to what the employee needs to learn and do on the job
- **T**ime-limited
  There is a clear beginning and end
- **E**ngagement
  The learner is actively involved, interested, and able to see progress
- **S**kill level
  The desired skill/knowledge level is specified
- **St**ructure
  Tools and processes for guidance, direction, and feedback

We suggest you use these criteria as prompts for designing the development assignment. As we illustrated above, they can remind you to address topics you might otherwise forget. Let's apply the criteria to one of the development assignments we discussed above.

Development Activity:
Review Recording of Practice (Dry-run) Presentation

***Specific*:** Review recording to identify specific strengths and areas to improve.

Measurable/assessable: Identify elements of presentation that were effective as well as ineffective in terms of what was said and how it was presented. For elements that could be more effective, identify alternative ways to present.

Achievable challenge: Doing the dry run and then analyzing the presentation.

Relevant: Given the development goal, this is directly relevant.

Time-limited: Must be completed before the next scheduled presentation.

Engagement: The process of reviewing the recording and identifying areas to improve ought to engage Susan.

Skill level: Specifically, handling difficult questions by answering quickly with a firm voice while looking at the audience.

Structure: The recording itself provides a means for Susan (and possibly others) to identify strengths and areas for improvement. She also could put together a checklist to use when reviewing the recording. This would ensure she addressed everything she wanted to address. If other people get involved in reviewing the recording (another example of structure) they also could use the checklist.

Another way to use these criteria is to evaluate proposed development experiences. An evaluation grid has been provided below. This is a simple way to quickly assess how well your proposed development assignments meet the criteria. Based on the assessment, the manager and employee would review the grid and determine which activities to keep and which to modify or discard. Sometimes an activity like reading a book can be useful even if it is a low challenge.

Some people will be comfortable using the evaluation grid. Others may find the level of detail off-putting. The evaluation grid is just a tool. The point here is to make sure the development assignment will help you accomplish the goal. If the grid doesn't work for you, assess the development assignment elements in whatever way works best.

As discussed above, the extent of the manager's involvement will vary. At a minimum, the manager should be involved enough to understand the development assignment and its various elements and be able to use that knowledge to be an effective broker and obtain support and/or arrange for assignments with other managers.

Development Assignment Experience Evaluation Grid

1. Write the list of possible Development Activities/Experiences in the left-hand column.
2. Rate each Activity/Experience as LOW, MEDIUM, or HIGH. This is specific to the individual and his/her Development Goal. Make additional notes as needed.
3. Select the most helpful Development Experiences. Consider how different Experiences might be combined to strengthen the development assignment.

Key DA
Steps
Factors

Elements Possible Experiences	Specific	Measurable Assessable	Achievable Challenge	Relevant	Time-Limited	Engage-ment	Structure
Read books, articles to anticipate questions, issues, etc.	Medium	Medium	Medium	Medium	Low	Low-Medium	Low
Solicit input and questions from 2-3 potential audience members before finalizing presentation	Medium	High	Low-High Depends on Interviewees	High	High	High	High
Prepare a dry run presentation	High	High	Medium	High	High	High	High
Conduct/record dry run with co-workers. Distribute presentation in advance so they can identify difficult questions to ask during the presentation	High	Medium	High	High	High	High	High
Review and analyze recordings of dry-run presentation; modify delivery, answers, and overall presentation as needed	High	Medium-High	High	High	High	High	Medium-High

Identify Possible Constraints

The next step is to put together the development plan. Before proceeding to the plan, it's essential to know whether the development assignment is realistic for your organization. More specifically: are the necessary resources available? We define resources very broadly. It includes time, money, people, facilities, organizational support, knowing who to talk to and being able to do it, schedules and competing priorities, etc.

To use the example above:

- Will Susan's co-workers have enough time to review her presentation and sit-in in a dry-run?
- Will other people she intends to interview be available?
- Is there equipment available to record and play back a presentation? This is not something for a cell phone. The resolution should be good enough so that manager and employee can clearly see facial expressions as well as broader gestures.

The development assignment will change depending on the answers to these questions. It is not enough to identify what seem like reasonable elements of a development assignment. Each organization and individual has limits. If the development assignment is pushing up against the limits, make sure there is a way around them or change that part of the development assignment.

Summary

In general terms, we suggest three steps:

1. Choose development activities/experiences that will help you reach the goal.
2. Make sure there are a variety of activities/experiences to enable acquisition of knowledge and application.
3. Make sure the development activities and the overall assignment meet criteria for an effective development assignment.

More specifically:

- Brainstorm development activities—use 70-20-10 to help identify possible activities.
- Use the SMARTESST model to fill in the details of the development activity.
- Evaluate the development activities using the SMARTESST Grid.
- Select the Experiences that seem most likely to help the individual learn.
- Refine Experiences as needed.
- Combine Experiences to design a development assignment that will help the individual achieve the Development Goal.
- Evaluate the development assignment for resource requirements and potential barriers to make sure it is realistic

FORMS

Your Development Goal:

Possible Development Activities:

1. _____

2. _____

3. _____

4. _____

5. _____

6. _____

7. _____

✳ *Note:* You should use a variety of development activities. To help you do that, sort the development activities you have identified into the chart below.

70—20—10: Development Experiences/Activities		
70 Assignments, Application, Experience	**20** Other People	**10** Traditional Learning Approaches

Development Assignment Experience Evaluation Grid

1. Write the list of possible Development Activities/Experiences in the left-hand column.
2. Rate each Activity/Experience as LOW, MEDIUM, or HIGH. This is specific to the individual and his/her Development Goal. Make additional notes as needed.
3. Select the most helpful Development Experiences. Consider how different Experiences might be combined to strengthen the development assignment.

YOUR Development Goal:

Elements Possible Experiences	Specific	Measurable Assessable	Achievable Challenge	Relevant	Time-Limited	Engage-ment	Structure

Your Development Assignment

After evaluating possible development experiences, please list those you intend to use for your development assignment.

SMARTESST is intended to capture in one place all the elements needed to prepare the development goal, the development assignment, and the planning goal.

Criteria	Development Goal	Development Assignment	Planning Goal
Specific *Clear purpose and outcome in concrete and/or behavioral language*	X	X	X
Measurable/Assessable *Can be behavioral; quantitative must be meaningful*	X	X	X
Achievable challenge *Achievable but stretches the employee beyond usual performance level*	X	X	X
Relevant *Applies directly to what the employee needs to learn and do on the job*	X	X	X
Time-limited *There is a clear beginning and end*	X	X	X
Engagement *The learner is actively involved, interested, and able to see progress*		X	
Skill level *The desired skill/knowledge level is specified*	X	X	
Structure *Tools and processes for guidance, direction, and feedback*		X	

Chapter Five

PREPARE THE DEVELOPMENT PLAN

"Ok," said Joe. "Now we've got enough information to make a plan."

"Yeah," said Susan. "We've got the goal and the things I need to do to reach the goal."

"So now you can figure out things like resources you need, what might get in the way, and what to do about that."

"Right," said Susan. "Anyway, I know how to do all that. The main thing that worries me is the milestones. I mean, assessing how I'm doing. I've got my main development activities and those could be milestones, except I still need to figure out how I'll know when I've accomplished what I'm supposed to accomplish with each of them."

This is called the planning step, but the planning process actually began with the first step. In reality, this is the part where you spell out how to implement the development assignment. The end result will be a schedule that reflects the planning process and provides answers to these familiar planning questions:

- What is the goal?
- What actions/development activities are needed to achieve the goal?
- What are barriers to implementation and actions to overcome the barriers?

- What are the milestones?
  —How will you assess/measure to demonstrate that you have reached the milestone?
- What roles will the employee (learner), manager, and others play?
- What resources (time, money, people, equipment, etc.) are needed to support implementation?
- What is the deadline/due date?

The primary focus in this chapter will be on Susan's concern about assessing her progress and knowing if and when she's accomplished her milestones. Other than a brief sample plan and some general guidelines for constructing a development plan, provided at the end of this chapter, there will be little or no discussion on building a schedule or how to answer the other questions above. We assume you know how to do that.

Development Plan Milestones and Steps

In a project plan, a milestone is a point that signifies completion of a project phase. Reaching a milestone usually leads to a status meeting to discuss whether there has been sufficient progress per some pre-determined criteria. The project manager, project implementer, and others assess progress and determine next steps such as moving forward, addressing problems that have emerged, re-scoping part of the project, etc.

The same should occur when someone reaches a development plan milestone. There probably won't be a product, but there will be a need to hold a status meeting to mark and assess progress and determine whether to proceed as planned or alter course. We will discuss the status meeting in the next chapter. The milestone should represent a point in the plan where the employee knows and/or is able to do something he or she didn't know or couldn't do before.

Development activities will fall into one or both of these categories:

- Do you know it? (gaining knowledge)
- Can you do it? (developing a skill/changing behavior)

These are what you will assess.

We caution against overly ambitious milestones. It's better to start small and then adjust based on your experience. We also caution against assuming that implementation of your development plan will work without hitches. Just like any other plan, it is quite likely the development plan will require some adjusting as implementation progresses.

"Ok," said Susan, "so how do I assess how I've done?"

"I think you already know," said Joe. "What do you think?"

"How would I know?" asked Susan. "I don't have a Ph.D. or anything like that."

"This really isn't rocket science," said Joe. "You assess things every day. Everyone does. And you make decisions based on the assessment."

As Joe said, we all assess other people and events every day. Here are some examples:

"I expect people to be on time and Fred is not."

"Emma always lets me know when there is a potential problem."

"I really liked the way Ben handled himself with those difficult clients."

These might not be "scientifically" precise assessments, but they have the essential elements of any assessment:

- What is being evaluated has been clearly identified—*e.g. Fred's punctuality.*
- The criteria are clear—*e.g. no surprises when there is a potential problem.*

The more specific you can be the better. For example, we could expand the description of how Ben handled the difficult clients to: *Ben is very skilled at handling clients who want to redefine project scope without wanting to extend the schedule or pay more.*

"I get it," said Susan. "It's like last week when we were talking about that project with Kevin and I explained why it didn't go so well."

"Exactly," said Joe. "And no Ph.D. required."

"Why don't we try this on some of your development activities?" asked Joe.

Susan showed him this list.

- Read books and articles to anticipate questions, issues, etc.
- Solicit input and questions from two to three people in potential audience before finalizing presentation.
- Prepare a presentation for the dry run.
- Conduct and record a dry run with co-workers, who would receive the presentation in advance so they could identify and ask difficult questions during the presentation.
- Review and analyze the recorded dry-run presentation and then modify delivery, answers, and the overall presentation as needed.

"This looks like a sequence or framework for your plan," said Joe.

Susan agreed.

"So where do you want to start?" asked Joe.

"How about the beginning" said Susan?

"Alright," said Joe. "What do you want to accomplish?"

"Well, like it says, I want to anticipate questions, issues, and so forth" said Susan. "Now you're going to ask me how I'm going to know if I've done that. And I'm not sure I will know until the actual presentation."

"That makes sense," said Joe. "So what are you going to do instead?"

"I don't know," said Susan and paused. Then she looked at Joe and said, "It's ok if you just tell me the answer. Do you know it?"

"Maybe," said Joe. "I'm not sure. I think I know one or two things I would do. But I don't know if it's the right answer."

"So what is it?" asked Susan.

"I want you to come up with ideas too," said Joe. "Why don't we brainstorm? I'll get us started. And let's use the white board. Seeing the ideas helps me think of others." Joe paused. "The basic idea, I think, is to identify activities that ought to lead to the outcome you want. So, for example,

- *Did you talk to the right people?*
  —I'll set up some meetings for you if that would help.
- *Did you try out questions and topics on a few people who could be in the audience?"*

"Ok," said Susan. "This is a little different than what I thought I should do, but how about this:

- *Did I find the answers to the questions I couldn't answer before?*
- *Did I do some research and then go back to some of the people I talked to before to see if I had answered their questions?*
- *Am I making sure I'm aiming at the right knowledge level? Let's not leave out SMARTESST."*

They both smiled. Then Joe added another item:

- *"Did you look at where we're going as a company and the implications for what you're going to talk about?"*

Joe paused. "I think that's a pretty good list," he said. "My assumption is that if you do those well, you'll be able to anticipate what people will ask. Or at least you'll have enough information to come up with an answer pretty easily. Does that make sense?"

"Sure," said Susan.

When you can't describe the desired outcome with enough specificity you still can assess the process for reaching that outcome. This approach is not at all unusual. Many types of audits—quality audits in hospitals and manufacturing, for example—are assessments of processes that should lead to desired outcomes. If they don't, one or more processes will need to change.

Notice too that Joe is suggesting Susan return to the people she initially interviewed to see if she is getting at the questions they might have. This is an example of the experiential learning cycle, which we will discuss in the next chapter.

As for the other development activities Susan plans, she will be able to identify the outcome she wants very specifically and behaviorally.

For example, when it comes to answering questions, she can say that she wants to:

- Look directly at the audience.
- Speak at a moderate level—loud enough to be heard, but not much louder.
- Answer without hesitation. If a pause is necessary, demonstrate control by announcing the pause—e.g. "Before I answer, let me think about that for a moment."

When it comes to the presentation, she can say that she wants to:

- Refer to the Power Point slides but not read them—behaviorally this could mean that she will turn to the slides, gesturing with her hand, and then turn back to the group.
- Speak relatively quickly as a means of conveying energy and enthusiasm.
- Vary her tone of voice.
- Use minimal gestures with her hands.

We recognize that words such as moderate, to describe the volume of her voice, and minimal, to describe gestures, are open to interpretation. However, when Susan views the recording of her practice presentation, she can clarify and specify further.

✱ Note: See the very end of this chapter for another example—Steve's development plan.

More Examples

As we mentioned above, development activities and milestones focus on one or both of the following:

1. Gaining knowledge—do you know it?
2. Developing a skill/Changing behavior—can you do it?

Here are examples of outcomes and the specific knowledge (**K**) and skill/behavior (**S/B**) development activities that will be used to accomplish those outcomes. (Not all the activities needed to achieve the outcomes are listed.)

what   How - Specific

Outcome	Activity/Activities
Learn and be able to apply the company's procedure for returning merchandise	Review procedure online (**K**) Shadow person who handles this (**K**) Describe steps in procedure (**K**) Discuss to clarify possible areas of confusion (**K**) Implement with supervision (**S/B**) (**K**)
Learn and be able to use the approval process for capital improvements	Interview person who handles this to get overall orientation (**K**) Observe each step and discuss with appropriate person to clarify questions and prepare for practice(**K**) Practice and receive feedback. (**S/B**) (**K**)
Learn and be able to apply active listening skills e.g. paraphrasing, asking clarifying questions	Attend a workshop on this topic (**K**) (**S/B**) Apply what was learned and receive feedback (**S/B**) (**K**) Revise approach based on feedback and do it again (**S/B**)
Learn and be able to use three gestures that are effective when making a dramatic point in a presentation	Observe presentations to identify desired gestures (**K**) Practice and record (**S/B**) Review with subject matter expert and determine how to improve (**K**)

Notice that each development activity has a specific purpose, each of these outcomes is concrete, and the activities lead directly to those outcomes. The manager and the employee should not have to guess about whether the employee has met the outcome.

SSD? (handwritten note in left margin)

This is important for the next step in SSD, which is the status meeting. Having specific concrete criteria contributes to the success of the project status meeting for at least two reasons:

Status ~ meetings (handwritten note in left margin)

1. Using concrete criteria can decrease—but not necessarily eliminate—defensiveness. That is because the conversation is about something both the manager and employee agree actually happened.

2. The employee/project implementer is responsible for reporting on the status of the project—the development plan. Self-assessment often is inaccurate, especially when the assessment is or can be subjective. With concrete outcomes, it is or should be a simple question of whether or not the criteria were met.

As in most project status meetings, the project implementer—the employee—is responsible for a progress report. But both the employee and manager should understand and agree ahead of time on how progress will be assessed. If they don't, the status meeting might not work.

Planning Guidelines and Suggestions

Review & Reassess (handwritten note in left margin)

Here are some development-planning suggestions. Because people have different levels of expertise one person's milestone may be another person's development goal. For example, in one case developing active listening skills could be the development goal. In another, the goal might be to develop negotiation skills, which incorporate active listening.

Most of the steps in the development plan will be development activities. The rest will be for logistical purposes. For example, reserving a room to practice making presentations is for logistical purposes. Practicing and getting feedback is for development.

Each step in the plan should move the plan forward. This is another way of saying that each step should have a purpose or outcome. As you work out the specific steps to implementation you probably will re-examine and redefine specific tasks that were originally in the plan. This can be for many reasons—you might have thought of a better way, people and/or other resources might not be available (or different people and/or resources may be available), you've had to reduce the scope of the project because of other priorities, etc. This process will continue as you implement the plan, review its progress, and adjust it as needed. It is one of the reasons change orders were invented.

Here are some areas to keep in mind as you plan:

<u>Consult others</u>: Chances are there are others in the organization who have already learned what the employee intends to learn. Find those people. Ask them for advice. Ask them to describe what they did, how long it took, the barriers they faced, and how they overcame the barriers. Consider their answers when identifying necessary resources and laying out steps, a schedule and milestones.

<u>Tasks with a purpose</u>: Each step in the plan should advance the employee toward accomplishment of the development goal. This means that the employee (and manager) should know and be able to articulate what he or she is supposed to learn or accomplish at each step. Many people will organize their learning around that goal. If the task is to read a book or participate on a special committee or attend a workshop or gather information from a subject matter expert, the employee should know specifically what he or she is supposed to learn.

<u>Task/step duration</u>: Most people are not very skilled at estimating. Do you recall the last time the due date for a task was weeks away and you waited because you had plenty of time —and then discovered you'd waited too long? It's better to break things into small, relatively short tasks. This makes it easier to estimate correctly. It also makes it easier to change direction if things don't work

out as planned because you won't have spent weeks or longer going down the wrong path.

<u>Knowledge work is rarely linear:</u> You cannot schedule knowledge work with the same precision as more tangible work, such as the overnight delivery of a package or building a house. We suggest check-in or status meetings more frequently than might be done with other projects—every two to four weeks. The relatively brief time between check-in meetings necessarily means that the learning will be focused and incremental and that the manager will be able to control the project more easily.

<u>Build in necessary structure:</u> Remember structure in SMART-ESST. It's important to make sure that various mechanisms for guidance, direction and feedback have been built into the plan. These will help the employee stay on track, assess progress, and be successful. Obviously, the more skilled someone is in the area where skills are being developed, the more targeted and less frequent this needs to be.

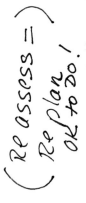

<u>Be prepared to re-plan:</u> As noted while discussing the development assignment, issues related to resources and organization priorities often create obstacles for development assignments and the need for re-planning. But re-planning is not unique to development or learning and managing the change process is a critical project management responsibility. No-one can predict the future with 100% accuracy. That's why it's important to use the planning phase to identify what could go wrong.

Summary

Here are questions we suggest the employee (and manager, as needed) answer to create a development plan. Not all of the answers will appear on the schedule. However, what does appear should reflect those answers.

- What is the goal?
- What actions are needed to achieve the goal?
- What are the barriers to implementation and the actions to overcome them?
- What are the milestones?
    —How much do you anticipate will have been learned by each milestone?
    —How will you assess/measure that learning?
- What roles will the learner, manager, and others play?
- What resources (time, money, people, equipment, etc.) are needed to support implementation?
- What is the deadline/due date?

Development activities and milestones focus on one or both of the following:

- Gaining knowledge—do you know it?
- Developing a skill/Changing behavior—can you do it?

Each development activity should have a specific concrete outcome and move the plan forward. When criteria are concrete you can see them, hear them, touch them, count them, etc. They are not about who the employee is; they are about what the employee does or says or both. The employee should not have to guess about whether he or she has accomplished the outcome.

It is essential to build in structure—the **ST** in SMARTESST. It provides the guidance, direction and feedback needed to stay on track and be successful. It enables the employee to be able to tell how he or she is doing or has done.

Answers Questions from p.63 the pool of questions

EXAMPLES AND BLANK FORMS

Example: **Susan's Plan**

- *Goal?*
  —Identify at least two questions and their answers for each major point in the presentation; deliver the answers in a way that demonstrates knowledge and control of the material

- *Actions needed?*
  —Prepare plan, meet with boss, arrange for observers, brief them on desired feedback, practice alone & for boss, present, record & review recording, etc.

- *Barriers to implementation; actions to overcome?*
  —Barriers: other work priorities, permission to record, time to practice, identifying people to provide feedback, patience with learning curve and frustration

  —Actions: work with manager to arrange schedule; identify and invite people to observe practice presentation, ensure there are specific measures of progress, identify people to provide feedback—ensure they know what you want and how to provide it

- *Interim assessment measures for major milestones?*
  —Utilize assessment measures established with development activities

- *Roles?*
  —Manager: Work with employee to arrange schedule to enable him/her to engage in development activities; arrange for meetings with others in organization who can provide expert input and feedback; establish status review meeting

schedule with employee; review and confirm/revise expectations established at the beginning of this process

—Employee: Establish workable plan and realistic milestones; do the work needed to reach milestones and development goal; review and confirm/revise expectations established at the beginning of this process

—Others: subject matter experts provide expert input; selected meeting participants provide focused feedback

- *Resources?*
  —Time, opportunity to present dry run, people to observe, equipment to record and review

- *Due date?*
  —6 weeks from beginning of effort

On the following page is a detailed project plan with the typical categories needed for such plans. Some will find that doing such a plan is very helpful. Others will not, especially if they are uncomfortable with detail and detailed plans. In the end, the manager and employee need to decide what would fit the situation best.

However, there are good reasons for having a detailed written plan:

- The preparation process can help an individual work out the steps and sequence needed to reach the milestones and ultimately the goal.
- It can make it easier to demonstrate what resources are needed, when, and why.
- If the plan is followed, it can be easier to discuss what was done, the underlying assumptions, and what happened.
- Having everything laid out in a plan can help ensure that details are not forgotten.

Susan's Project Plan

Development Goal: Identify at least two questions and their answers for each major point in the presentation; deliver the answers in a way that demonstrates knowledge and control of the material.

Actions	Outcome: Assessment Criteria/Measures	Who Does What	When to be Done	Resources
Review this plan; establish meeting schedule with boss.	2-3 people whose opinion is important	Me, Joe	WK 1	1 hour
Identify people to speak with who will be part of the next presentation audience; schedule meetings. Get Joe's help if needed.	Identify 3-5 topics to investigate	Me, Joe as needed	WK 1	In 1st meeting with boss;
Meet with these people to identify topics and questions of interest.	Information sources identified	Me, people to interview	WK 1-2	
Identify information sources to provide answers— books, articles, other people. Obtain material, set up meetings (Joe may help arrange).	Confirmation to move ahead	Me, interviewees, Joe, others as needed	WKs 1-2	
Status Meeting: To review progress; determine whether Joe has anything to add to findings; discuss next steps—who to invite, etc.	Answers to questions obtained	Me, Joe	WK 2	1 hour
Review books/articles, etc.; meet with subject-matter experts if needed.	Confirm satisfaction with answers and/or process	Me, Joe might help	WKs 1-3 May extend beyond wk 3	2-20 hours
Touch base with interviewees to ensure I can answer their questions—and to see if they have more. Continue to review material as needed.		Me, interviewees	WKs 2-3	1-2 hours
Identify/invite people to practice presentation. Explain purpose; that it will be recorded and they will be asked to provide feedback.		Me, audience participants	WK 2	1 hour
Reserve room and equipment.		Me	WK 2	15 minutes

Action	Notes	Who	Week	Time
Prepare/modify presentation (assumption is that I will modify a draft presentation).		Me	WKs 2-3	2-3 hours
Give each participant, including Joe, a copy of presentation and request they identify challenging questions.		Me, audience	WK 3	15 minutes
Status meeting: To review progress, discuss modifications to presentation, discuss any problems and possible solutions	Confirmation to move ahead			
Deliver and record presentation. If unable to answer question(s) find answer(s). Debrief presentation focus on development goals.			Wk 4	2 hours
Review recording of presentation—alone and then with Joe and/or no more than 2 others.	Answering questions look for: • Look directly at the audience • Speak at a moderate level—loud enough to be heard, but not much louder • Answer without hesitation. If a pause is necessary, demonstrate control When presenting look for: • Refer to the Power Point slides but not read them • Speak relatively quickly as a means of conveying energy and enthusiasm • Vary tone of voice		Wk 4	Alone—2-3 hours With others 1-2 hours
Based on review - modify delivery, answers, and the overall presentation as needed.	Complete modifications			3-6 hours
Status meeting: To review modifications and preparations for final practice before delivery to group.				1 hour
Practice delivery again—with a peer. Record and review.	To ensure all issues have been addressed		WK 5	1 hour for presentation 2 hours for review
Finalize presentation.	Ready for presentation		WK 5	1 hour

Planning Questions for Development Plan

These are questions to answer when formulating the development plan. Not all answers will appear on the plan. However, what does appear should reflect those answers.

What is the goal?

What is the deadline/due date?

What actions are needed to achieve the goal?

What are barriers to implementation and actions to overcome the barriers?

What are the milestones?

What roles will the learner, manager, and others play?

What resources are needed to support implementation?
(Resources = time, money, people, equipment, etc.)

Development Planning Form

Treat and track Implementation as a Business Project Implementation Plan. Be sure to include progress review meetings:

Actions	Outcome: Assessment Criteria/Measures	Who Does What	When to be Done	Resources

✳ **Note:** *For those who would like to see another example of development planning, here is what Steve will be working on. If you are not interested, please skip to the next chapter.*

Example: Steve

As noted earlier, Steve' development goal related to delegating more effectively. Here is more background information along with his goal and development activities.

Background: On occasion, Steve would lead projects. Steve is not a manager and the people working on the projects reported to other people and usually had other priorities. When he delegated work, results were mixed. The people who received the assignments usually did not do everything that Steve wanted or the way he wanted it. Additionally deadlines were missed more than once. They were not happy and Steve was frustrated and uncertain about how to correct the situation.

After some investigation on his own and talking with Joe, Steve realized that he wasn't doing enough to generate a commitment to his projects. More often than not, he simply would delegate after a brief discussion in which he did most of the talking. He also resisted in engaging in discussion about why he wanted something done a particular way. He approached other people's schedules in a similar manner and usually did not work with the people to whom he was delegating to accommodate other assignments and priorities.

After discussions with Joe, Steve concluded that he needed to be able to negotiate the schedule since he could not dictate it. He also needed to be able to describe what he wanted the other person to do and why. People tended to resist being told how they should do something—especially if they knew how to do it well enough to be delegated the assignment in the first place.

Development goal: ensure commitment to schedule and outcomes when delegating—especially to people who do not report to you and who have other assignments they must accomplish.

Development activities:

1. Identify at least three reasons the other person (the person to whom you want to delegate) would benefit from this assignment. If you can't think of benefits, identify at least three reasons this person would accept the assignment.
   a. Assessment: the three reasons (These should be realistic and assessed first by Joe. Final assessment is with the person being delegated the work.)
2. Identify at least three reasons this person would resist this assignment and how to counter the resistance.
   a. Assessment: the three reasons and how to counter each (These should be realistic and assessed by Joe. Final assessment is with the person being delegated the work.)
3. Identify the minimum and maximum you want to delegate
   a. Assessment: clearly described as assessed by Joe
4. Describe the desired outcome and why it should be achieved. If the task should be done a certain way, prepare a full explanation
   a. Assessment: Clearly written descriptions understandable to others
5. Clarify the other person's current work load and obligations
   a. Assessment: result of discussion; write it down and confirm agreement with other person
6. Collaborate with other person to prioritize this assignment, modify the assignment, if needed, and establish a due date
   a. Assessment: Completion of a plan both agree on
7. Agree on mutual expectations, including performance feedback
   a. Assessment: Written list of expectations both agree on

Let's highlight several of the assumptions Steve and Joe have made:

- The first four development activities will provide Steve with information that will be useful during his discussion with the person he wants to delegate to.
- Steve will treat these four development activities seriously and not just think of something at the last minute.

- Steve knows how to collaborate, be flexible, etc. If he didn't we might see more specific behavioral development activities related to things like soliciting input or active listening. Just because he knows how doesn't mean he will use it.

Notice that the development activities can be divided into two phases:

1. The first phase would include the first four activities.
2. The second phase would include the last three.

A status meeting could be held between the two phases.

There are very clear outcomes for each of the activities as well as criteria for assessing whether the activities have been completed. In general, evaluating knowledge acquisition is a matter of comparing what someone knew before a learning experience with what they know after the experience. Although we often think of knowledge acquisition coming from school, a workshop, or a book, learning experiences are not limited to formal "official" learning settings.

If the employee can identify three reasons the other person would benefit from the assignment, then the employee has accomplished that step in the plan. The same applies to the next three steps. During the meeting between the two phases, Steve and Joe would discuss the outcomes for items 1-4. They would consider modifying or enhancing them, and would discuss how to apply that information to the forthcoming meeting Steve will have with the person to whom he wants to delegate. Subsequent status meetings should be used to review how helpful the information was and what would have made it better.

Development activities 5-7 have more than specified outcomes. They also specify processes for reaching those outcomes. To achieve the development goal, Steve can't simply dictate priorities. Steve and the person he is delegating to must discuss and clarify, etc.

It is the structure (the **St** in SMARTESST) that will enable Steve to determine how he is currently doing, or has done in the past. As a reminder, structure provides the guidance, direction, and feedback Steve needs to stay on track and be successful. Here are structures that Steve and his manager have used:

- The specific outcomes for the development activities are elements of structure.
- The meeting between the two phases.
- Any preplanning Steve and the manager do prior to his meeting with the person being delegated to.

Here are some examples of other things Steve could do:

- Prior to the delegation meeting or at the beginning of it, Steve could explain why he wants to handle delegation differently. He could say that he wants to collaborate, prioritize, etc., and wants to briefly check in about this during the meeting to see if he is on the right track. Steve is not likely to get detailed behavioral feedback. Most people don't do this very well unless they have had a lot of practice. That's why it's helpful to check in a few times during the meeting.
  —We strongly suggest not waiting until the end of the meeting to discuss how the meeting is going. Memories are short and a discussion at the end of the meeting is likely to be hurried and not very helpful.
  —One other note: Steve might want to just try out the development activities without telling the person he is delegating to. But there is a good chance this person will not notice any changes—at least for a while. So it would be more useful for Steve to enlist this person's assistance.
- Steve could ask if he could record the meeting for later review alone, with the manager, or a subject matter expert. He might also want to review it with the person he is delegating to if he or she is willing and there is enough time. (If they are in different locations and the meeting is held via the internet, it should be easy to record it.)
- Steve could get permission to have someone observe the meeting, with the explicit goal of providing feedback.
- Steve could consult with a subject matter expert after the meeting.

Chapter Six

IMPLEMENT THE PLAN: CONDUCT THE STATUS MEETING

All the work from the previous chapters comes together in this step—implementation. So it seems appropriate to do a brief review. The basic premise of Supported Self-Development is that a manager has the skills needed to support the development of an employee if that manager knows how to work with others to: set goals, formulate a workable plan to achieve the goals, engage in problem solving, and conduct status meetings to check status and determine course changes if they are needed. Within that context and using project management as the framework, here are the steps we've seen Joe and his employees take.

1. The manager and employee should *clarify expectations and respon-sibilities.* Briefly: the manager's job is to support project planning and implementation; arrange for resources and assignments, as needed; conduct and participate in the status meetings, and to provide feedback—or ensure that it is provided.

   In most cases, the employee has primary responsibility for planning and implementing the project—the development plan. (The exception would be if the employee doesn't have enough experience.) The employee is also responsible for providing status reports on the project.

   By providing status reports, the employee is, of course, providing feedback on his or her own performance as well as es-

employee Driven

planning
implement
updates

74

tablishing the foundation for the status discussion. This is easier—though not necessarily easy—when the plan milestones are specific and concrete and others can see whether they have been achieved. As we noted at the end of chapter 3, self-assessment can be very difficult.

2. Identify the _development goal._ There can be a variety of reasons for the goal—to prepare for another assignment/promotion; to address a performance problem; to fill a current or anticipated skills gap in the organization; etc. Once identified, the goal itself should be **S**pecific, **M**easurable/Assessable, **A**chievable, **R**elevant, **T**ime-bounded, and the appropriate **S**kill level should be specified. (**SMARTS**)

3. Design the _development assignment_. The development assignment includes all the above elements and adds two more, **E**ngagement and **St**ructure. (**SMARTESST**) Engagement refers to making sure the development assignment is something the individual will find involving. Structure refers to the different types of support needed to accomplish the development assignment. At a minimum that includes a feedback mechanism. But it also could include things like planned conversations with subject matter experts and written procedures and other job aids.

Engage
Structure

4. The _implementation plan_ spells out how the development assignment will be accomplished and therefore how the development goal will be achieved. The implementation plan is essentially a project plan with measureable or assessable milestones where the employee and manager will assess and discuss progress and modify the plan as needed—as would happen with any project plan.

Notice that the development goal, development assignment, and the implementation plan milestones should be **S**pecific and **M**easurable/Assessable. As with any project, there is a fundamental reason for emphasizing this: when a goal or development assignment or milestone is specific and measurable/assessable both the employee and manager know whether it has been achieved. If it hasn't been achieved, this specificity is the basis for the status discussion and any problem solving and corrective action that may follow. If it has been achieved, this could be the basis for identifying successful practices that the employee might want to continue and others might want to adopt.

With the above as context, our focus will be more on learning from project implementation than implementation mechanics—but sometimes they overlap, especially when things don't go as planned. Here's an example:

"I'm not sure we have much to talk about," said Susan. "I'm not getting the information I need from those people we identified."

"They're canceling on you?"

"No. They're there and they're nice enough I guess. But it's like they suddenly got stupid. I ask a question and they don't have anything to say. They mostly just look at me."

"So how did you set it up," asked Joe?

"What do you mean? I sent an email to arrange for the meeting and I explained what I wanted to talk about in the email," said Susan. "Then when I got there, I had to remind them about the email. And about what I wanted to know."

"You sound frustrated," said Joe.

"I am," said Susan. "Some of these people are the same ones that got me last time. It's hard to believe they don't have some question or two that's going to derail me."

"So you think they're out to get you?"

"Not really," said Susan. "But it feels like it. It's just that they have these great questions when I'm doing a presentation and nothing now when I need their help."

"So what do you want to do?" asked Joe.

"You know you're pretty frustrating yourself," said Susan.

"Remember when we all talked about this?" asked Joe. "Everyone agreed that you guys were going to solve the problem or at least come up with some solutions. I'm supposed to help. Just like any other project. But you know I don't have a bag full of answers any more than you do. This is your project. I'm happy to help. But do you really want me to tell you what to do?"

"Sometimes," said Susan. "But you're right. And, you know, I think I've probably behaved like they did more than once. Someone wants my input and I'm just not thinking about it when they ask—even if they tell me when they're going to meet with me."

"So what's the difference between that and when they're asking you questions in the presentation?" asked Joe.

"Well they're thinking about it the whole time I'm doing the presentation," said Susan. "So maybe these interviews aren't such a good idea."

"Maybe," said Joe, "but maybe not. You wouldn't necessarily be able to get all of them to a dry run. But now you might be able to get some of them."

"Yeah," said Susan. "Or maybe I should just sit with them one-on-one and go through the presentation."

"Good idea," said Joe. "I think that's better than my idea. Or maybe you should try both . . . "

Joe and Susan have been discussing project status. A problem has come up and they have identified a possible solution. This is a learning process. We have intentionally chosen an example that is not specifically aimed at "learning" to illustrate that learning happens all the time. It's not a special event. There were four steps involved:

1. acting
2. thinking about what worked and what didn't
3. deciding what to do about that
4. identifying a new plan or revising the old one

Action Learning Cycle

You also could call the process "trial and error," or "plan, do, check, act," or "after action review" (the military's term). They all are basically the same. It is also called an experiential learning cycle. Here is a diagram describing it. (Adapted from work by David Kolb.) We will be building on it.

Experiential Learning Cycle

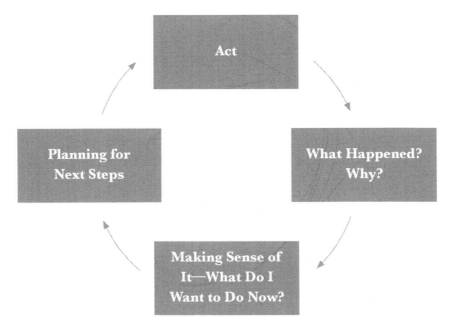

All of us engage in this learning cycle—usually without focusing on it. But because the purpose of a development assignment is to learn or enhance knowledge and skills, we suggest you use questions based on this model to guide discussion of the development assignment during the status meeting. You can make up your own questions. But here are some suggestions:

- **Act**
  —What step(s) in the plan are we addressing?
  —What did you do?

- **What happened? Why?**
  —What did you expect to learn/accomplish?
  —What did you learn/accomplish?
  —What challenges did you encounter? What did you do to address them?

- **What do I want to do now?**
  —What remains to be done?
  —What would you stop doing, start doing, continue?

- **Planning next steps**
  —What needs to be done—based on plan and status review?
  —What challenges do you anticipate? How do you plan to address them? What support might be needed?

The Status Meeting and Feedback

The project status meeting is not a performance appraisal meeting. It should focus on the four steps above.

The employee is first to provide a project status report or feedback on him or herself. The manager should listen; ask questions about plan and progress; engage in problem solving, as needed; ensure that they have identified lessons learned; and provide positive and/or developmental feedback as needed. (We will discuss feedback guidelines below.)

If the employee's development assignment is in another work unit, the manager may want to discuss the employee's work with the individual in the other work unit who is assisting with the development assignment. This is no different than what a manager would do with a direct report who has a matrix assignment.

Because the employee goes first in the status meeting, he or she has the opportunity to set the framework for the discussion. The employee should use specific examples to show that he or she accomplished the milestone and/or describe obstacles and actions that were taken to address them. Or, if the employee is having difficulty accomplishing the steps in the plan, he or she should say so and suggest an alternative, if that is appropriate.

Knowing the employee's assessment will help the manager gauge his or her focus. If the employee has accomplished the milestone the discussion then can touch on what the employee learned, problems encountered and how they were solved and next steps. If the employee hasn't, the discussion can focus on what the employee learned, problem solving and/or possibly re-scoping the project. You can expect that giving and receiving feedback will be a key element of these discussions.

We know that many managers are uncomfortable with delivering feedback and consequently do their best avoid it. That is one of the reasons we want the employee to report first. We also know that employees are often uncomfortable reporting difficulties they may be having regardless of the type of project.

Just as projects would fail if team members did not honestly discuss what is working and what needs to work better, supported self-development will not succeed if the employee is afraid to report and discuss what has worked well and what hasn't. Learning stops when people are afraid to reveal anything less than perfect results. That is why it is important to recall the mutual expectations we suggested that the manager and employee develop at the beginning of the project.

"How was the dry run?" asked Joe. "By the way, I'm sorry I missed it. I couldn't get out of that trip. Will you send me the recording? I'll take a look tomorrow."

"Do you want to wait until after you see it?" asked Susan.

"I guess we could. But I'd rather hear what you think first. That way I can focus any feedback I have."

"OK. I guess that's what we said we'd do." said Susan. "Anyway, it mostly went ok. I mean I got some difficult questions and they didn't throw me even if I didn't know the answers. So between this and the one-on-ones I

did going over the presentation I feel like I'm going to be better prepared. And I don't think I'll get as much push back as before. You know, because I think this could be helping me build some support too."

"That's great," said Joe. "Anything you'd do differently? Anything didn't go the way you hoped?"

"Well," she said, "I'm not very good at receiving feedback. I'm not sure I'd tell you this. But you're going to see it anyway. Of course some of them aren't very good at giving feedback. Bill said that he expected more of me. But when I asked him for some detail he acted offended. Of course he's not one of my biggest fans, which is why I invited him. But what am I supposed to do with feedback like that?"

"I'd probably just say thank you and move on," said Joe.

"Even if he could tell I wasn't being completely sincere?" asked Susan.

"If you're going to be sarcastic," said Joe. "Just move on to someone else. There's no upside to picking a fight. I know from personal experience."

"Sounds like a good story," Susan smiled.

"It depends who's telling the story," said Joe. "There wasn't much that was good about it. Just take the high road and move on." Joe paused then said, "Anyway, I don't want to get off track. Tell me more about the feedback. Is there something about the presentation that could have been better or is it just how you handle feedback?"

"Probably both," said Susan. "You know, I asked people to give me feedback on whether my voice got really soft or I looked down. And it turns out I did both even when I wasn't getting hard questions. Especially not then since I made sure I looked right at the person asking when I responded. It's weird. I'm not happy about it. And I got defensive when people told me I was doing it."

"So how can I help?" asked Joe.

"I don't know," said Susan. "They were being specific and behavioral the way you're supposed to be when you give feedback. And I know I was sup-

posed to not take it personally. You know, listen and ask questions to get a better understanding. But I just wanted to tell them they were wrong. I didn't. But I wanted to. And they were right. I looked at the recording." She paused. "I hate watching myself."

"I know how you feel," said Joe and paused. "Look, just because people follow the rules doesn't mean you won't react. But at least you know what they're talking about and you can check it out; not like with what Bill said."

"So what do I do?" asked Susan.

Joe was quiet and looked at Susan.

Susan looked at Joe then said. "Ok. I know. What do I think I should do? Right?"

"Right. But I don't think there are any magic quick fixes."

Their conversation continued. Eventually, Susan decided that she was going to focus on one behavior at a time—not looking down. They both agreed that if she focused on just one thing, she'd have a better chance of accomplishing it. She also decided that she would practice not taking things personally and focus instead on understanding what people were trying to tell her. She and Joe agreed this would take a lot of practice.

Feedback Rules—giving feedback

As Susan and Joe discussed, the basic rules for giving feedback are to:

- be specific and concrete or behavioral
- not use evaluative language

As we have seen, being specific and concrete are important in many ways—not just for giving feedback. When being specific and concrete we have to take care to avoid evaluative language, which sometimes seem specific and concrete but really are not. Words like brilliant, assertive, confident, stupid, a disappointment, etc. are examples. There are additional rules that we summarize at the end of this chapter. But if you can do these things, chances are you will deliver accurate feedback that is more likely to be accepted—and easier for you to explain.

maybe yes or maybe no

Numbers

We discussed the use of numbers earlier. We bring them up here because numbers seem concrete and specific but often they are not. They are just numbers—unless you can explain or demonstrate what the numbers mean. This applies equally to grades. And when you do explain or demonstrate what the number or grade means, that explanation should be the starting point for a discussion about what has gone well and what could be done better and how.

One other point: because numbers appear to be precise, some might believe that development can be precise. Usually, it's not. For example, we have heard some talk about development as simply a matter of raising a rating from 3.5 to 4.0—just a half point: easy. Unless you know what behavior(s) to change and how much (what exactly constitutes that half point?), this sort of talk is misleading at best.

Receiving Feedback

When you are receiving feedback, your primary goal is to understand it. That means you:

- ask questions to help your understanding
- practice active listening
- avoid getting defensive, which is another way of saying don't take it personally

Remember just because you understand the feedback does not mean you have to agree with it. Sometimes it's easier not to take it personally when you remember that.

Maintaining motivation

Learning is not always easy or smooth. Inevitably, the learner will come upon something that is difficult to master. Or the learner might face other issues such as time pressures. Whatever the reason(s), there are two related questions the learner must be able to answer:

1. Is the goal important enough that he or she will persevere?
2. How will the learner continue to motivate him or herself in difficult circumstances?

There can be many reasons for a goal to be important enough to stick with—you want to get promoted; you want to keep your job; you see that you are making real progress toward reaching your goal; it's something you've always wanted to learn, etc. Often the more challenging a goal is, the more motivated the individual is. Whatever the reason is for you, find it. As for the second question, we all have had times in our lives when we kept ourselves motivated when it would have been easier to quit. What did you do?

No one can create motivation in another person. But the manager can help create a situation in which the employee is more likely to motivate him or herself. The manager can do this by meeting the expectations we discussed earlier. More specifically, by:

what Leader Does?

- Demonstrating that he or she believes the development assignment is important
- Ensuring that the development goal is clear
- Providing feedback—about the task and the process of accomplishing it; not about the individual receiving feedback
- Being an effective broker
- Helping the employee to manage the obstacles in the workplace—such as schedules

Summary

When the project is a development plan, implementation is about putting the development plan into action and learning from what happens. In other words, it is not just about doing. It also is about stepping back and learning from what worked and what could have worked better. The experiential learning cycle provides an easy way to think about the basic steps in the learning process. Because of that, it also provides an easy to follow discussion outline for the employee's report and the status meeting.

The purpose of the status meeting discussion and feedback is to identify and discuss what happened, what worked and what didn't, and what the next steps should be. The employee goes first. The milestone or outcome should be specific and observable. Consequently it should be fairly straightforward for the employee to demonstrate whether he or she reached the milestone. If the employee did not reach the milestone he or she should be able to discuss problems encountered and actions taken to address those problems.

Both employee and manager should focus on specific observable behavior. The employee should focus on what he or she did or did not do. So should the manager. Reaction to that behavior is important but not by itself. Telling someone they made you angry is not helpful feedback unless you can tell that person what he or she did that led to your anger.

Both manager and employee should follow the rules for giving and receiving feedback.

Rules for giving feedback include:

* Be specific about what the employee did, didn't do, or could have done. Focus on behavior—what someone says or does. If you can't see it or hear it, chances are you're not being concrete and behavioral.
* Use objective non-judgmental language. Your evaluation or interpretation is as much or more about you than the person receiving feedback.
* On a day-to-day basis, try to deliver feedback as close to the event as possible. If someone is receiving feedback on something he or she did months before, the feedback might not be understood very well and its importance could reasonably be questioned.

Rules for receiving feedback include:

- Listen to understand. Don't take it personally.
- Summarize in your own words what you heard to make sure you understand. Repeating what you heard verbatim demonstrates a good short term memory. It does not necessarily demonstrate understanding.
- Clarify by asking questions and by asking for examples and stories to illustrate.
- Remember: Understanding feedback is not the same as agreeing with the feedback.

Suggested Steps for the Status Meeting Discussion

- **Act**
  —What step(s) in the plan are we addressing?
  —What did you do?

- **What happened? Why?**
  —What did you expect to learn/accomplish?
  —What did you learn/accomplish?
  —What challenges did you encounter? What did you do to address them?

- **What do I want to do now?**
  —What remains to be done?
  —What would you stop doing, start doing, continue?

- **Planning next steps**
  —What needs to be done—based on plan and status review
  —What challenges do you anticipate? How do you plan to address them? What support might be needed?

Chapter Seven

CONFIRM WHAT WAS ACCOMPLISHED, IDENTIFY LESSONS LEARNED & NEXT STEPS

"How do you think it went?" asked Joe.

"I'm actually surprised," said Susan. "I think it went pretty well."

"I agree," said Joe. "I looked at the recording. Well done! Your voice was clear. You didn't look down or mumble. And you handled all the questions without much difficulty."

"Yeah, I think I did pretty well. Thanks. There were a few times I could have stumbled if there had been a few more follow-up questions. But no one pushed. So I still have to work on my knowledge."

"You seemed knowledgeable to me," said Joe.

"Maybe," said Susan. "Or maybe they didn't ask any follow-up questions because they were just being nice."

"I doubt that," said Joe. "You did some other things that helped—like building support ahead of time so people knew where you were coming from."

"I guess so," said Susan. "Building support ahead of time feels very political to me. I've always felt uncomfortable about that in the office. Like I shouldn't need to do that."

"Think of it this way," said Joe. "Sometimes people just need extra time to get used to an idea. Ok?"

"Ok," said Susan. "So I think we're done with this development project. What do we do now?"

"The same as we do at the end of every project," said Joe. "Review the lessons learned and figure out what we can do better the next time."

Project Conclusion

Sometimes projects just end. There is no final meeting, or process for a final accounting or to capture what was learned. We suggest a final meeting to do just that. This probably won't be the last development assignment for the employee. And it probably won't be the last time the manager will be supporting an employee's development. Having a final meeting or follow-up to assess what was learned benefits both the employee and the manager.

If the manager and employee have been holding regular project status meetings, this step will be very familiar. In essence, it is one last status meeting. However, the discussion will focus much more on what has been learned and, presumably, not much on project status. At this point, both the employee and manager should already know whether the employee can reach—or has reached—the development goal.

Unlike other projects, the conclusion of Susan's particular project will not require the release of resources and other typical closure activities. Similar to other projects, it would be easy to simply acknowledge that the employee had achieved the development goal and move on.

However, like any other project, we think it is important for the employee and manager to consolidate the lessons each has learned. For an employee, this is an opportunity to understand how he or she learns best, the challenges they faced, and how they addressed those challenges. For a manager, this process allows him or her to understand what worked well and what could have worked better with regard to supporting the employee's development plan. And for both manager and employee this is about how well each met the expectations established at the beginning of this process.

It would be best if the employee and manager prepared answers to the following questions individually and then met to discuss their answers. It's helpful to do this because the manager and employee probably will have different perspectives. It also would or could be useful for each to hear the other's perspective. However, we recognize that if this conversation occurs at all, it is more likely that it will be based on the employee's answers and that the manager will select those items they choose to share with the employee.

Sample Questions

Here are questions to use as the basis for discussion during the follow-up meeting.

Add or adjust as needed:

Employee

- Have you accomplished the development goal? Please demonstrate.
- Did you learn/accomplish what you expected to? Explain. What else did you learn that would be or has been useful?
- How can you apply what you have learned to your work and to your next development opportunity?
- Can you perform the overall desired outcome? If not, what more do you need to learn? (Remember, the development goal is often an element of the overall desired outcome.)
- What are possible next development steps?
- Please look at the tasks listed below. Given what you know now, what would you continue to do the same? What would you change? How?
  —Establishing mutual expectations
  —Meeting/adjusting mutual expectations during the development process
  —Creating the development plan

—Implementing the development plan

—Status meetings

—The overall development process

- Would additional support have been helpful? If so, please describe what and why. What resources are needed for this additional support?

Manager

- Given what you know now about the tasks listed below, what would you continue to do the same? What would you change?

—Establishing mutual expectations

—Meeting/adjusting mutual expectations during the development process

—Creating the development plan

—Implementing the development plan

—Project status meetings (feedback, problem solving, re-planning, etc)

—Providing support (arranging for assignments, introductions, discussions with the employee, etc)

- What can you apply to supporting future development assignments?

Chapter Eight

SUMMARY

Here is a summary of Supported Self-Development and the steps we have described above.

What is Supported Self-Development?

Supported Self-Development (SSD) is an approach to development based on the idea that a manager has the skills to support the development of an employee if that manager has basic project management skills—knowing how to work with others to: set goals, formulate a workable plan to achieve the goals, engage in problem solving, and conduct status meetings to determine whether and what course changes are needed.

The purpose of supported self-development is to enhance or develop job-related knowledge and/or skills.

Manager and Employee Roles

The employee's role is to plan and implement the project—the development plan—and to have primary responsibility for his or her own learning. The manager's role is to act as a project manager for the employee's development plan and to provide necessary support. Both are accountable for the results.

91

Responsibility for Learning

Generally speaking, people learn what they want to learn and don't learn what they don't want to learn. Self-development does not mean that individuals have to figure out everything by themselves or that managers have no responsibility. *Most people can't figure out everything themselves.* They need various types of support. That is the manager's role and it is essential. And that is why this is called Supported Self-Development.

Implementing Supported Self-Development

To implement Supported Self-Development follow these steps:

1. **Agree on who will do what:** clarify mutual expectations
2. **Choose the right things to work on:**
   a. Identify the knowledge/skills needed to accomplish what you want or need to accomplish
   b. Define the development goal
3. **Choose the right ways to work on the development goal:** Design the development assignment
4. **Prepare the implementation plan and identify what to assess or measure.** Have a development plan with *observable* outcomes that can be assessed or measured
5. **Implement the plan:** Assess progress regularly; adjust the plan as needed
6. **Confirm that the goal was accomplished.** Identify lessons learned and next steps

✳ **Note:** Here are brief descriptions of what to do in each step.

1. **Agree on who will do what:** clarify mutual expectations.
   To do this, the manager and members of his or her team should have a meeting in which:
   • The manager clearly describes how he or she is approaching employee development using SSD.

- The employees answer the following questions:
    —*What should my manager reasonably be able to expect of me during the development process?*
    —*What should I reasonably be able to expect of my manager during the development process?*
- The manager answers the following questions:
    —*What should employees reasonably be able expect of me during the development process?*
    —*What should I reasonably be able to expect of my employees during the development process?*
- The manager and employees discuss their answers and agree on what each can and should expect of the other.

2. Choose the right things to work on. Define the development goal.

    This is a process of going from the general to the specific.

- Identify the development area and desired outcome(s). These can be general areas such as improving delegation skills, or presentation skills, etc.
- Distinguish between an overall goal—like making effective presentations—and what someone needs to learn or develop in order to accomplish that overall goal. For example, you don't just learn "effective presentation." There are a variety of things you should know and/or be able to do to create and deliver an effective presentation. For convenience, we call these *performance elements.*
- Identify and list the performance elements and determine which need to be developed.

    The development goal is based on the performance element(s) you have chosen. To define the development goal, we suggest you use the familiar acronym **SMART** and then add one more letter, **S**. **SMARTS** stands for:

- **S**pecific: *Clear purpose and outcome in concrete and/or behavioral language*
- **M**easurable/Assessable: *Includes mechanisms to determine progress*
- **A**chievable challenge: *Achievable but stretches the employee beyond usual performance level*
- **R**elevant: *Applies directly to what the employee needs to learn and do on the job*
- **T**ime-limited: *There is a clear beginning and end*
- **S**kill level: *The desired skill/knowledge level is specified*

3. Design the development assignment.

In general terms, we suggest three steps:

1) Choose development activities/experiences that will help you reach the goal.
2) Make sure there are a variety of activities/experiences to enable acquisition of knowledge and application. Remember 70-20-10.
3) Make sure the development activities and the overall assignment meet criteria for an effective development assignment.

The criteria for an effective development assignment are contained in the acronym **SMARTESST**. To form this we take **SMARTS**, add two more elements and slightly rearrange the letters. Here are definitions of each element.

- **S**pecific: *Clear purpose and outcome in concrete and/or behavioral language*
- **M**easurable/Assessable: *Can be behavioral; quantitative must be meaningful*
- **A**chievable challenge: *Achievable but stretches the employee beyond usual performance level*
- **R**elevant: *Applies directly to what the employee needs to learn and do on the job*
- **T**ime-limited: *There is a clear beginning and end*
- **E**ngagement: *The learner is actively involved, interested, and able to see progress*

- **S**kill level: *The desired skill/knowledge level is specified*
- **St**ructure: *Tools and processes for guidance, direction, and feedback*

4. Prepare the implementation plan and identify what to assess or measure.

Have a development plan with _observable_ outcomes that can be assessed or measured.

Development activities and plan milestones focus on one or both of the following:

- Gaining knowledge—do you know it?
- Developing a skill/changing behavior—can you do it?

Here are suggested questions to create a development plan. Not all answers will appear on the schedule. However, what does appear should reflect those answers.

- **What is the goal?**
- **What actions are needed to achieve the goal?**
- **What are barriers to implementation and actions to overcome the barriers?**
- **What are the milestones?**
    - —How much do you anticipate will have been learned by each milestone?
    - —How will you assess/measure that learning?
- **What roles will the learner, manager, and others play?**
- **What resources (time, money, people, equipment, etc.) are needed to support implementation?**
- **What is the deadline/due date?**

Each development activity should have a specific and concrete outcome that should move the plan forward. When criteria are concrete you can see them, hear them, touch them, count them, etc. They are about what the employee does or says or both. If the concrete outcomes include numbers or grades, make sure you can define what the numbers or grades mean in very concrete terms. Otherwise the number or grade is just an abstraction. The employee should not have to guess about whether he or she has met the outcome.

As you design the development plan and activities, it is essential to build in a mechanism that provides the guidance, direction and feedback needed to stay on track and be successful. This is structure (the **ST** in SMARTESST). It enables the employee to be able to tell how he or she is doing or has done.

5. **Implement the plan: Assess progress regularly; adjust the plan as needed.**

The project status meeting is the setting for assessing progress. It is a key element in SSD. As in any project status meeting, the employee goes first and reports on the status—what has gone well and what needs to go better. The manager asks questions and helps solve problems. We suggest using the following steps, based on the Learning Cycle, as a guide for the status meeting:

- **Act**
  —What step(s) in the plan are we addressing?
  —What did you do?
- **What happened? Why?**
  —What did you expect to learn/accomplish?
  —What did you learn/accomplish?
  —What challenges did you encounter? What did you do to address them?
- **What do I want to do now?**
  —What remains to be done?
  —What would you stop doing, start doing, continue?
- **Planning next steps**
  —What needs to be done—based on plan and status review?
  —What challenges do you anticipate? How do you plan to address them? What support might be needed?

An effective status meeting requires that both the manager and the employee be able to discuss what worked well and what did not. Supported self-development will not succeed if the employee is afraid to report and discuss actual results. Learning stops when people are reluctant to reveal anything less than perfect results.

Delivering feedback effectively is important; so is receiving it well. There can be many rules for both. Of all those rules, we suggest you focus on the following:

Rules for giving feedback include:

- Be specific about what the employee did. Focus on behavior and objective language—what someone says or does. If you can't see it or hear it, chances are you're not being concrete and behavioral. For example, saying that someone interrupted me when I spoke describes behavior. Saying that person is rude might be an accurate description of my evaluation of the behavior, but it does not describe the behavior. Telling that person to stop being rude, will not tell that person what behavior to change.

Rules for receiving feedback include:

- Listen to understand. Do not take it personally.
- Summarize and reflect back what you hear.
- Clarify by asking questions and by asking for examples and stories to illustrate.
- Remember: Understanding feedback is not the same as agreeing with the feedback.

6. **Confirm that the goal was accomplished. Identify lessons learned and next steps.**

In addition to demonstrating, in whatever way makes sense, that the goal has been accomplished it is important for the employee and manager to consolidate the lessons they each have learned.

- For the employee, this is about challenges he or she faced and how those challenges were addressed, what the employee would do the same and do differently next time, and what he or she has learned that can be applied to the next development goal and plan.

- For the manager, this is about what worked well and could have worked better in supporting the employee's development plan and what he or she can apply when supporting other employees.

- And for both manager and employee this is about how well each met the expectations established at the beginning of this process.

SUPPORTED SELF-DEVELOPMENT BASIC PRINCIPLES

There are six principles underlying this approach to employee development.

1. <u>There must be a good business reason for the employee's development effort.</u> That is because the employee's development is an investment of organization resources. The employee is learning something he or she needs to know in order to accomplish a real job task. The employee's manager should be able to clearly define the business reason for the development effort and be able to use it to get support from his or her manager. Just as the project manager and employee in charge of implementing a project are accountable for a project and its outcome, the manager and employee also should be accountable for the development plan and its outcome.

2. <u>Learning comes primarily from experience.</u> We try things out, watch others, ask questions, apply classroom learning, etc. In a work setting, that means development assignments, focused learning on the job, etc. But self-development *does not* mean that individuals have to figure out everything by themselves or that managers have no responsibility. Most people need some type of support. It is the manager's role to provide that support.

3. <u>Each individual is in charge of his or her own learning.</u> That is because no person can learn for another. Individuals can be directed or required to learn and many will. But there are lots of examples of people who chose not to learn—perhaps because they weren't interested or because it was too complicated or because they did not see the relevance to their job or for some other reason. It is difficult to force someone to learn something they don't want to learn. But most people do learn what they want to learn. And when an individual has the support they need, great things can happen.

4. <u>Desire is necessary but not sufficient.</u> There is no magic. The learning process can be frustrating. Persistence and motivation are necessary, as well as an appreciation for what is possible. It is important to remember that there are some things that we never will master as well as we'd like.

5. <u>Attitude counts.</u> Both the manager and employee should believe that the employee can develop his or her abilities. This sounds obvious, but not all managers and employees act as if they believe this. For example, there is the manager who acts as if the employee isn't capable of learning something new or cannot improve their skills. Then there is the employee who is afraid to try something new for fear of looking less than completely competent. The fact is all of us probably have learned something we weren't sure we could. And all of us probably know someone who learned something we weren't sure they could. (Adapted from Carol Dweck, 2006.)

6. <u>Learning is not a one-time event.</u> When a plan needs to be modified because something wasn't anticipated, the decision to modify the plan is the result of learning. This regularly happens with projects. An individual goes through a similar learning process. (Adapted from David Kolb.) There are four steps:

- an individual acts
- they reflect on the results of the action
- they decide what they want to do differently
- they re-plan as needed

A key implication is that aiming for perfection is fine but expecting it is unrealistic. Managers should encourage their employee(s) to do the best possible, learn from the experience, and do better next time.

SUGGESTIONS FOR FURTHER READING

The Talent Code, Daniel Coyle

Talent is Overrated, Geoff Colvin

Informal Learning, Jay Cross

Mindset, Carol S. Dweck, Ph.D.

Self-Theories, Carol S. Dweck, Ph.D.

The Road to Excellence, K. Anders Ericsson

How to Talk So Kids Can Learn, Adele Faber and Elaine Mazlish

Learning to Learn, Marcia Heiman and Joshua Slomianko

Experiential Learning: Experience as the Source of Learning and Development, David Kolb

Practice Perfect, Doug Lemov, Erica Woolway, and Katie Yezzi

Fundamentals of Project Management, James P. Lewis

Developmental Assignments, Cindy McCauley

A Manager's Guide to Self Development, Mike Pedler, John Burgoyne, and Tom Boydell

Self-Directed Learning, George M. Piskurich

Job Aids & Performance Support, Allison Rossett and Lisa Schafer

5 Steps to Expert, Paul G. Schempp

Self-Regulated Learning, Dale H. Schunk and Barry J. Zimmerman

The Genius in All of Us, David Shenk

Enhancing Adult Motivation to Learn, Raymond J. Wlodkowski

ACKNOWLEDGEMENTS

When this project began, there were three of us. I want to thank Deborah Pettry and Nancy Lorsch for their help in shaping the concepts that are the foundation of this book. I especially want to thank them for their input as the book crept toward completion.

Marla Bradley provided feedback and other help, which I greatly appreciate.

Martin Wilcox and Melanie Arrowood Wilcox provided much appreciated advice and encouragement. Thank you.

Several people read the book or sections of it and provided useful feedback. They include Steve Keleman, Marty Rubin, Nolan Pike, Glenn Akin, Brenda Post, Anne Berlin, Paul Pinegar, Chuck Murphy, Kathy Rubin, and Lynn Rhodes.

I want to thank Jennifer Deal for her timely advice and feedback.

I want to thank my editor, Kate Russillo, and book designer, Greg Smith.

And finally, I want to thank my parents each of whom in their own way helped make this possible.

Made in the USA
San Bernardino, CA
03 May 2013